# Natural
# Pathways
# of Recovery

**Also by Pam Moore**

The Kingdom Within - A Six Week Journey

Unhook and Live Free

Show Me the Way How to Unhook and Live Free

*To all who work and strive to end the suffering.*

# Acknowledgments

We have had the good fortune to be influenced by many great teachers and leaders over the years. We are grateful to everyone who offered ideas and wisdom to us over the years, with a special recognition to Terrance Gorski (1949-2020). He was a man ahead of his time and gave the world of recovery such valuable information about both relapse and Post Acute Withdrawal.

While working in treatment with inpatient and direct care we met and learned from many gifted caregivers of all types. Our co-workers in the field have greatly influenced our work.

We salute all those who are working to help others. We appreciate our colleagues so very much. It takes a great deal of strength and courage to work in a field where we lose too many.

We have had the privilege of working with thousands of people who helped us to understand what is really happening. Thank you for the gift of working with you while you got better.

We thank those who spent their time and effort to do friendly edits of this book, especially Dan, Clay and Danny. We want to thank Sandra Slate, who has helped us illustrate and edit this book. Thank you to Shauna Moore for the inspiring painting the cover is based on.

We want to give our deep appreciation to Jim Burke. His support and encouragement to us to keep on the path means more than words can say. And we press on.

# Table of Contents

# Introduction

*In the middle of difficulty lies opportunity.*

Albert Einstein

Most people get better. They just do not get better in the way we think they should.

It can be very frightening and overwhelming if you or someone you love has a problem with the use of alcohol or drugs. There is reason for hope, most people do recover. The often-quoted studies of negative outcomes such as jails, institutions or death are extremely unlikely and they are not the usual results of Substance Use Disorders (SUDs). This does not mean your situation is not serious and important. It also does not mean that those drastic outcomes could never happen to you or someone you care about. However, there is cause for hope if we can understand what is actually happening and determine the best course of treatment.

It is a human trait to seek relief from pain and problems. People have been trying to find a way to address and alleviate these issues for as long as we have recorded history. Much of that time humans have used mood-altering substances in some form as a part of that effort. It could be considered successful use when we get relief from short term substance use. Even long-term substance use, resulting in few significant consequences, can be considered successful use. However, unsuccessful use is characterized by any continued substance use despite severe negative consequences, or the threat of negative consequences. There is no real problem if one acknowledges the negative consequences and changes behavior. Real problems arise when the solution of using mood-altering substances continues despite severe negative consequences. We must then use the term Substance Use Disorder or SUD to characterize a personal behavior that has become dysfunctional.

It is for this reason that we have spent our careers working with, questioning, and researching substance use disorders. We have spent thousands of hours working with people with substance abuse disorders, and with their families over the course of thirty years. We were taught in the traditional method of recovery that the only way to recover was to go to 90 12-Step Meetings in 90 days, read the Big Book, and work the steps with a sponsor. This method worked for some people, but not all. So, we wondered, questioned and researched. This book will explain what we learned in a way that is easy to understand and utilize.

In this book, we explain how to look at recovery from substance use disorder (SUD) in diverse ways and why that will be helpful. We will introduce you to the Multi Modal Recovery Process © and the Star Matrix Assessment System©. Treatment should be unique for the individual's problem and issues. We designed our first concept of the Star Matrix in early 2002. At that time, it was too complex and complicated. We left it on the drawing board, focusing instead on how to simplify the Star Matrix into a working model. Slowly, over time, we were able to turn it into a simple and direct model.

Originally, the Star Matrix was a four-pointed star which included biology/genetics; frequency, intensity and duration; co-existing disorders; and consequences. As we worked with the model in practice, we realized two important issues that enhanced the model. Shame became a big part of the consequences. The other factor we realized over time was how much physical issues could play into a person's substance abuse disorder, as well as affect their recovery. This could include physical traumas to the body, disease, age, as well as the effects of post-acute withdrawal on a person. There is a more in-depth discussion of these findings in a later chapter. As a result of our findings, we added a fifth arm to the Star Matrix.

From the Star Matrix we developed the Multi Modal Recovery Process. Since there are many ways to look at what the words "alcoholic/addict" mean, we realized we must also have many methods to treat the problem. We will discuss how these two methods combined help to define the term alcoholic/addict in a new way. This way of thinking about, and understanding, both the problem and the solution offers additional insight with a much more hopeful way forward for those who need help.

*Pam and Steve Moore*

# How We Got Here

*The secret of change is to focus all your energy not on fighting the old but on building the new.*

*Socrates*

## How We Know About SUD (The History of Addiction)

We know a great deal about the use, and misuse, of mood-altering substances. The simple reason is that it has been happening for a very long time. There have been problems with the overuse of mood-altering substances probably for as long as we have known about these substances. We have often wondered who discovered some of these – it would seem that in order to discover a leaf that will change your mood, someone had to smoke a lot of bad stuff that did nothing. However, our ancestors apparently persisted and now we know of, and have created, many substances that alter human moods at least temporarily. Some of these substances have produced relatively good results overall and some have reduced much human suffering (such as acute pain).

However, if we could look at history and literature with the intention of gaining a better understanding of the overall results, we could see that there have

1

been problems with the misuse, overuse and abuse of these substances for as long as they have been around. From that we could see something that might be called the "History of Addiction" even though we have not used this term for very long. We have used the term Substance Use Disorder (SUD), instead, for an even shorter time.

The most important question is why some people have significant problems with the overuse of substances while others do not. Why do some people continue to ingest mood-altering substances despite severe negative consequences or the threat of negative consequences? History could reveal that we have a significant amount of information about misuse, if for no other reason, than this – for as long as these problems have existed, there have been people looking for solutions.

As with many human problems, most of what we discover over time are possible solutions that do not appear to make it better, or maybe even make the problem worse. For example, shame, guilt and punishment do not seem to reduce the incidence of substance use disorders. If locking people up for drug and alcohol use was going to work, we would have noticed positive results by now. Drug prevention programs involving early intervention have not helped to reduce substance use problems much at all. We may yet design programs that are effective, however nothing we have done to date seems to have reduced the percentage of people who have the problems we now call SUDs. We have learned of many ways that are not helpful, and fortunately we have learned of methods that are effective. The question is, how do we put all this history and information to best use for you today.

We have been working in the field of recovery from substance abuse issues for over 30 years and we have been honored to watch thousands of people change their lives for the better. Recovery usually happens. It often happens slowly, occasionally quickly, but most people are getting better. It is not a simple or straight-line process, however there is movement forward and getting better over time which is encouraging and important to remember. Most people get better.

The majority of recovery models are based on extremely limited outcome information. It has often been reduced to an idea suggesting what works best for most people. Another idea used for many recovery models is it works if you work it. These two ideas combined have resulted in the notion that treatment professionals know what is wrong and know what to do about it. The only problem is getting people to do it. The SUD treatment profession has devolved into simplistic models of recovery for complex problems. Most have gone with the idea that they know what is wrong with you and what you need to do about it, therefore you must be willing to do what they tell you to do. Over time we have become certain that having simple solutions to complex problems is attractive but not effective.

*We must find a way to claim progress, not perfection, without that equaling permission to keep using.*

## What is Right vs What is Wrong

There is a tendency to pay more attention to slips and relapses than to forward progress. A person will abstain for 95 days and use for 2 days, and this is considered to be a failure. We must look at what they did wrong on the 2 days rather than how they managed 95 days of abstinence.

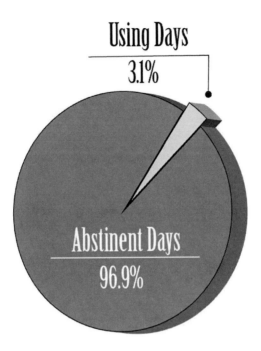

Working with substance abuse disorders is one of the few medical areas where absolute perfection is the only truly acceptable measure of success. We understand there is much fear when a person who has been abstinent uses substances again, even for a short time. The family of a person with a substance abuse problem has been traumatized by the constant fear of the negative consequences that comes along with a substance use disorder. It makes sense that anyone could be easily triggered into negative action based on the trauma that life with a substance abuser can create. The professionals around them tend to reinforce this belief that only perfection is acceptable in the area of abstinence.

We need to find a legitimate and workable way to claim progress, not perfection, without it equaling permission to continue to use. We do not endorse or encourage the continued use of mood-altering substances as a part of the solution, but we do acknowledge the reality that most people who attempt any form of sobriety do use again, even while trying to get better. Often they are getting better and we must find ways to work with the success and stop punishing the process. The recovery process is like a marathon. Each step matters but it is going to be a long race. We must learn to pace the progress in a more measured way.

## Studying the Problem for 30 Years

When we started working in this field, over 30 years ago, there was a rigid model of recovery that had been long standing. A user would go to inpatient treatment for 28 days, come home, go to 90 12-step meetings in 90 days, get a sponsor, read the "Big Book" of Alcoholics Anonymous, and perhaps try therapy and aftercare. There was not much time for family, work or life outside of the program. People were told it works if you work it, and for approximately 10% of people recovering from substance abuse (SUDs), this is true. Another 10% will return to treatment stating they did not work it and we then put them in the relapse category. We say they did not work it right, so they relapsed. However, for most people, recovery from substance abuse takes a much more complex trajectory than this simple linear path. There is a realistic and natural recovery process which is valid because it is based on the lived experience of persons who get better. Most importantly, the nonlinear and more complex path to getting better is what is happening with most people. There is a natural path of recovery for each person and we must find this with them while honoring and reinforcing the individual's own pathway to recovery. For many people this includes some years of harm reduction in the form of using less dangerous substances. There are people who end up coming off heroin or alcohol but continue to smoke marijuana. They are better, but not in the way we are taught to think. We do not advocate this approach, but we do acknowledge the reality of people's lives. We must find ways to honor the progress, not perfection, and to focus on the success that is moving people forward on their path.

# Painful Lesson

One of the authors, Pam, had a dear friend who she had been in treatment with named Kathy. After five years, Pam had stayed sober, and Kathy was a "chronic relapser" who had just found out she had cirrhosis and was going to die soon. She asked Pam very sincerely "why you and not me" (why have you been successful, but not me).

Pam thought about this for a long while. Kathy had followed the instructions more than Pam had. Kathy had willingly gotten a sponsor and Pam had tried but was unable to stick with one. Kathy had thoroughly worked the 12-steps, attended more meetings, and gotten on her knees and prayed every night. Pam worked hard too but not in the traditional way that Kathy did. So why Pam and not Kathy? It was not because Pam had tried harder, or better. Kathy had really tried. Pam could not answer Kathy's question at that time. We decided that it was important to keep asking ourselves that question and, in part, that is what this book hopes to answer. Why Pam and not Kathy? Shortly after this conversation Kathy died of complications from alcoholism. Her question lives on with us . . . we hope you can see that even though Kathy died still struggling with alcoholism, she did get better.

It is much harder as an addiction counselor to work with a person whose recovery looks messy and unpredictable, but the truth is they may be on a successful path. They are better, just in an unconventional way. In the beginning of our careers, there was a comfort in the belief that there was one way to recover so our only job was to convince the person with SUD to follow the path that had been designed for them in this strict model. It was the only path that often worked and there was no variance from the program.

Often, in primary treatment programs the model seems to work. Peer pressure would lead people to say, "Hi, my name is Pam, and I am an alcoholic/addict."

This felt like success to everyone. We thought we had admission and acceptance of the problem. Then all one had to do is teach the user how to work the 12-steps of Alcoholics Anonymous and then proceed to the very standard discharge plan of 90 meetings in 90 days with the person continuing in AA for the rest of their lives. After that, we thought they would remain sober and live happily ever after. But that is not what was happening. If only a small percentage of the people who were referred to 12-step meetings had continued to go for life, they would be holding meetings in football stadiums by now. And yet, the number of people attending 12-step meetings for all forms of SUD has remained stable for approximately the last 40 years according to the AA Center office figures. The model we were trained in just did not seem to work except for about 10% of the people in programs. We had built the entire model of what recovery should look like by the 10% we could observe.

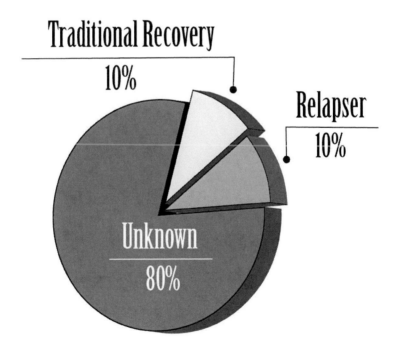

*Where are the remaining 80%?*

Research would show that another 10% of people return to treatment saying they did not work the program (non-compliant) and they had failed. This group was often called chronic relapsers. They were often told if they would just try harder the program would work for them, and then they would try harder, yet fail again. We blamed them for the problem. Substance abuse treatment is the only place wherein the program is never wrong. If you get better, it is because the program is great. If you do not get better, it is always your fault. Sometimes we would decide to characterize them as "constitutionally incapable" of getting better according to the standard program.

"Rarely have we seen a person fail who has thoroughly followed our path. Those who do not recover are people who can not or will not completely give themselves to this simple program, usually men and women who are constitutionally incapable of being honest with themselves. There are such unfortunates. They are not at fault; they seem to have been born that way. They are naturally incapable of grasping and developing a manner of living which demands rigorous honesty. Their chances are less than average.

There are those, too, who suffer from grave emotional and mental disorders, but many of them do recover if they have the capacity to be honest."

*(Page 58 Chapter 5 Big Book How It Works)*

We thought this meant the person was too weak-willed, stubborn, resistant or any number of character flawed problems. In other words, it was not about what we were teaching them, it was their fault for not trying hard enough. We always assumed the individual had failed to comply. We did not assume that we missed what was really happening to the person or that we were working on the wrong thing with this particular person. Instead, it would seem there was something wrong with the individual which prevented the program from working. It was difficult to question the model we had been taught.

For both of us, this approach started to look and feel wrong. We were disappointed and tired of it not working for so many people. People would be incredibly involved in the program yet still spiral or have small periods of time where they drank or used. They often felt they had done something wrong and needed to start over. Many people have a "white chip" collection which is the newcomer or start-over chip in many 12-step groups. Due to the belief that they "can't get it" – some give up.

With the Addiction Research Foundation, we were committed to studying the 90% of people who were neither compliant nor non-compliant and failing. What had happened to them? We began with confidence, believing this would be an easy problem to solve. We contracted with a national research firm and a local treatment center to allow us to follow a cohort of clients, with their permission, for five years to see what actually happens. Our belief was that since we were not associated with any particular treatment program, drug program or any other agency, people would be more likely to answer surveys on a regular basis. We spent many months and much money perfecting the questionnaire that was going to be the basis of this important survey. At the three-month interval we hired someone to email each participant. We did it once, twice, three times, resulting in an 8% response rate. We decided a personal phone call would help to create a better response. This put us up to a 9% response and we could never go beyond that. It was a big disappointment. We were very discouraged. We had spent so much time, money and resources and no matter how hard we tried we could not get a response from enough people to make this survey completely valid. It was heartbreaking, but we did learn something we should have already known. Outcome research is notoriously difficult and only the compliant 10% will respond.

On the side, we had developed an online survey created for social media allowing us to ask more basic questions for ourselves. These questions involved what people who had attempted to discontinue use were doing for their self-help. We received over eleven hundred responses from all around the world, and we found out some interesting things. One of the biggest lessons learned was that over time most people got better just not in the way we thought they would. Men and women seemed to use different methods to recover. While men tended to attend self-help meetings, women did not attend anywhere near the same rates. Women tended to use more solitary methods for sobriety such as journaling, yoga and friendships. And while some people thrived in 12-step communities, others were more drawn to their religion for sobriety. Others used non-traditional paths including meditation, acupuncture, amino acid therapy and an array of methods that would not normally be thought of as recovery. What we found is there was seldom one way to recover for these people, instead, many paths were taken. These revelations began to fit with our own experiences including the thousands of people we had worked with over the years. People did get better just not in the way everyone had imagined they should. We began to analyze and critique our own client files and their experiences with recovery. We then designed more specific surveys to better understand the details. The results have been startling and have changed the way we think about recovery from substance use disorders.

## People Get Better

Recovery or getting better takes many forms. We must be able to facilitate all forms of recovery with equal enthusiasm and expertise. We can not force people to get better the way we think they should.

# What Does Recovery Look Like?

A word about our research bias and our possible biases. We have been interested in outcome research for many years. Over the years we started to notice people were getting better just not in the way the industry said they should. People would figure out many paths and take many detours on their way through the recovery process. Rarely was there a straight arrow to a better life or recovery. Put simply: we wanted to know who gets better and why or why not. This kind of research is notoriously difficult and therefore one of our biases is to suspect ourselves of being biased in some ways. We include our own thinking here. At least partially to that end, we offer our personal stories next. These can provide some insight into our backgrounds and how that might influence our thinking and strategies for model development.

*Pam and Steve Moore*

# The Same but Different

*It is not our differences that divides us. It is our inability to recognize, accept and celebrate those differences.*

*Arthur Ashe*

■

To begin understanding that personal recovery or "getting better" is different, we the authors, Pam and Steve, are starting with our own personal stories. In many ways, our stories sound the same. We both used to excess, had many problems, went to treatment, attended one of the anonymous 12-step programs, worked the steps and stayed continuously abstinent thereafter. But when you look more closely, our stories are quite different – from our childhood histories, where and what we used, how treatment worked for us, the length of our treatment, our experience in the 12-step rooms, and much more.

There is not one way to recover. This is important because it illustrates the reason we should look at addiction differently. It is not simply about trauma, mental health, genetics, consequences, pain or avoidance, it is all of that and more, in very different degrees for each of us.

# Pam's Story

## In the Beginning

I was the 5th child of 6 children. We were economically disadvantaged and my parents struggled to make ends meet and struggled to emotionally connect with their children. There was every kind of abuse in my home and family growing up. My parents were alcoholic and my mom was also addicted to pills. You could say I grew up in extreme chaos and trauma. It took me well into my adulthood to understand the level of mental illness I grew up with. Due to the mental illness there was no one to trust and depend upon. To this very day my family mostly communicates with threats, manipulation and personal attacks.

In this life circumstance, my first use of a mood altering substance was on my 12th birthday. I drank at a friend's house, got sick, passed out and came to while being raped by her older brother. I felt deep shame about who I was. I soon was on a tranquilizer prescribed by a MD to help calm me down, and I learned two pills were better than one. I started sneaking swigs of alcohol out of the cabinet to calm my shame. By the 8th grade I was regularly consuming both drugs and alcohol. I barely graduated high school. At 19 I was pregnant for the first time. I lost my son in a traumatic way. He was born premature. I believed I should have done more to prevent it. I felt even more shame. I drank and used even more. I was arrested for drug use and thought it was just bad luck. I had trouble keeping a job and lived an aimless life. At 23 I married (an alcoholic of course) and became pregnant with my daughter. She also died. Neither died from my addiction as I quit drinking both times but both of their deaths increased my shame and pain and therefore my use.

After the death of my daughter, my drinking and drug use spiraled out of control. I ended up within a couple of years of her death a homeless IV drug addict charged with another felony and close to death. I literally fought wild dogs for baloney to keep from starving. I was disgusted with the person I had become. Yet, I remained stuck in the spiral I was in partially due to the homelessness, and partially because I did not believe I had what it took to be better. I accepted my eventual demise. I remember looking in a mirror and seeing death staring back at me. There was chaos all around me and I was chaos myself. I was beaten regularly, had guns pointed at my head. All of this happened with me believing there was something wrong with me and knowing somewhere in my head that it must be the substances (at least partially). At the same time I did not know it was substance abuse. It is interesting to me how a person can know it is substance abuse while not knowing at the same time. I would go back and forth even about homelesseness just being a free lifestyle choice to the terror of starvation and the extreme dangers that come with being homeless. Around this time of internal and external struggle,for the first time someone (a policeman), looked at me and called me an addict. It had occurred to me before but no one had spoken those words to me. People would say "your problem" or "your issue" but not that it was the drugs. My family had an easier time believing I had multiple personalities than for me to have drug addiction. So to hear the words out loud was powerful. It was that small niggling thought finally made real. I left the homeless camp I was staying at and he put me on a bus to Birmingham, Al where my parents lived.

# Recovery Begins

I moved in with my parents and started at a drug and alcohol clinic. My counselor (Tony) was kind and empathic with me. I saw on a bulletin board a flyer for a Cocaine Anonymous meeting and told my parents they said I had to go. I lied. No one had told me to go. My father took me to the meeting and waited in the parking lot so I could not run away. It was the first time I had been around people who were trying to not use drugs and it gave me hope. I attended meetings and therapy for about a month when a person at the meeting suggested I go to treatment as they did not think I was progressing in a way that was going to sustain sobriety. I went to an indigent care 45 day inpatient program that a member of the group helped me get into. I decided I would not use the substances for long enough to get my life back together (at least pot). I felt conflict and disbelief that I could never use drugs again. I learned a great deal in treatment, but the biggest thing I learned was that I was mostly on my own. I can remember the treatment counselor saying to me after meeting my parents that some of us have to be ok with not being loved and that we have to get better anyway. She pushed me to go to a halfway house after treatment because she felt my home life with my parents was too destructive. I agreed, only because there was no bed availability, and I thought it would look good to my counselor if I appeared willing. The night before I left treatment there was a mass discharge from the halfway house and they had plenty of beds. I felt stuck and went. I lived there for 6 months. It was very hard. The counselor at the halfway house would be sexually suggestive with me. The director was angry, bitter and emotionally abusive to the women that lived there. I stayed sober. My sobriety was not because of a profound change in my psyche. I was tired. I was starting to realize how much being homeless and the grief of losing my children had on me. I went back to seeing my original counselor (Tony). I attended Cocaine Anonymous and Alcoholic Anonymous meetings. I got a scholarship to college from Vocational Rehabilitation. So at six months sober I was working as a waitress and in college. By 10 months sober, I moved out of the halfway house and began trying to live life for the first time. I moved in with the counselor from the halfway house that had sexualized me. It was crazy and scary and a bad plan. She and her husband were using and physically beat one another constantly. I was scared. I realized what a bad plan I had made to move in with her. I realized I mostly just wanted to be out of the halfway house and to appear "better." A friend I attended meetings with suggested I apply for a job at his apartment complex as it came with an apartment as part of the pay. My car got a flat tire on the way to the interview. I changed the flat and went on to the interview late. I got a job as an apartment assistant manager because she liked my resilience to keep moving in the sign of adversity. For the first time in my life I moved into my own place.

# Pam Finds a Way that Works for Her

I tried getting sponsors and in my first two years of sobriety I had nine. (The counselor I moved in with was my first sponsor.) All nine ended up getting drunk. After that I decided that was not going to be part of my plan. I had a hard time with cravings (and remember my plan was not to stay completely drug free - I was going to go back to pot use at some point). I kept going to therapy and working hard on the issues surrounding the trauma of being raised with abuse and mental illness. I had very strong physical cravings for a very long time. I was not committed to not using - yet. Still, I would force myself to stay in my bedroom and wait for the cravings to pass. It was hard work. I did not decide to attempt long-term sobriety until after the two years sober point. I thought "Why not, I have come this far?" The time I had spent not using had changed my mind. I learned that even without a firm commitment to sobriety the commitment to giving myself time helped me develop the desire for long term sobriety. I did therapy twice a week both, individual and group. I started going to Al-Anon meetings (meetings for family members of people struggling with alcohol. Both of my parents were alcoholics) on top of other Anonymous meetings I attended. Regular AA and CA meetings did not feel like a great fit for me. I continued to go. I had bonds with the community and deep friendships. I worked the 12-steps multiple times. Still, I struggled with some of the concepts. I struggled with the belief that I needed to go to meetings for the rest of my life. That felt like a trap to me. By three years sober I was bored with hearing the same stories over and over again. I thought there must be more. I also struggled with even the idea of always identifying yourself as an alcoholic/addict every time you spoke. For me that seemed to miss the majority of who I was. I had worked the 12-steps as told. I still felt haunted by my childhood issues. I was attending both individual and group therapy. I believed I got more out of my therapy than I did in the self-help meetings. I was doing well in college and had new interests and a new life. At the same time I had friends and people I loved to be around at the meetings. I felt afraid of rejection if I did not go. I kept going to self-help meetings more for the friendships than because I had any belief they were keeping me sober. I started working in the treatment field and went along feeling discontent with the idea of attending meetings for the rest of my life. I married early in recovery to a man who could not stay sober. He was gay and in the closet. I think the burden of his secret kept him from finding peace. Living in the dysfunction of that much denial hampered my own abilities to grow. I was afraid that if I did not leave him I would not be able to continue with my sobriety. I ended up divorcing him a few months before I celebrated five years sober. I struggled emotionally but was excelling at college and work life. I got promotions at work. In college I was one of 25 people selected out of over a 1000 who applied to Advanced Standing in graduate school. (Today anyone with an undergraduate degree in Social Work can get into the Advanced Standing Program but back in 1991 it was a very big deal.) I went to graduate school. While in graduate school I met Steve. We were set up on a blind date by a mutual friend who knew we were both recently divorced. We developed a strong relationship built on our own and each other's continued growth that has maintained that commitment to this day almost 30 years later.

## Life Goes On

I completed my internship during graduate school while working at a local indigent treatment center. I admired my supervisor, Trevor, very much. I knew he was over 30 years sober and seemed to have an aura and peace about him no matter what was happening in his life. It was of interest to me that he had discontinued going to 12-step meetings after he had a couple of years sober. I talked with others there and almost everyone who worked there was 20 years and more sober and none of them went to 12-step meetings. They all had communities they were involved with, mostly church, but not 12-step communities. For the first time I learned there was more than one way to remain sober. They gave me hope for my own recovery.

At seven years sober, I started to disconnect from the "program" as the anonymous groups are called. Steve and I have stayed connected to the recovery world through our work. I have seen the 12-steps work for many people. I believe it has been a miracle for them. I am so appreciative that there are 12-step meetings. I support people attending 12-step meetings. It was not a good fit for me. I have not attended a 12-step meeting in over 25 years. I also have not used a mind altering substance since September 9, 1987. I have kept my own community and support system. I have stayed in therapy. I have worked on my early trauma for years. I have continued to work on my recovery - just in a way that fits who I am. My plan has changed over the years many times. What has remained and morphed at the same time is the need for community and continued growth on my part. My recovery today looks nothing like it did in the beginning. It has grown with me.

# Steve's Story

---

## What Happened

Near the end of 1989, my choices, mistakes and problems were really catching up with me. I was in daily survival mode which meant that every day, my main job was to find a way to get enough mood-altering substance to live. Mostly I had to try to find enough money to get what I thought I needed to be able to perform in the world. I was far down a path of denial and self-delusion about what I could get away with. I was always robbing Peter to pay Paul with a plan to get it together and straighten everything out. I told myself that I could pay everything back tomorrow if I could only get enough for today. It all ended when my employer, who was also my best friend, had to fire me for stealing from him. He drove me home in a company car which was no longer mine and said goodbye, and good riddance.

I was left with no car, no job, no money and no answers for my life except to find a way to use some today so I could fix it all tomorrow. My options were limited, and I considered all of them. I thought of walking to a drug store to rob it or stealing from someone else. But I really felt terrible and didn't think I could pull it off. It was not a moral decision. It was a failure. I did not have it in me, and so I was defeated in my only real plan. I laid on the floor and decided I was just going to lay there and die. I laid there trying to will myself to let go and die, but I didn't. I had to get up and try something else.

## It Works if You Work It

Somehow, I knew about Narcotics Anonymous and I found a phone number to call. Someone called me back and a guy named Matt agreed to meet me

20

that night at a meeting place called "We Do Recover." This was my first 12-step meeting of any kind. It was a very cold and dreary night and I recall arriving at a very rundown building in a rundown part of our city. I guess I was too sick and despondent to be aware of my fears. I was early and walked to see a scary looking guy making coffee. He turned around and said "welcome," while giving me a hug that surprised me. I had no idea what to do but I didn't ask, I just followed the next person into a room where over the next hour I heard the words "addict" and "fuck" more times than I had ever heard them in my life. It was cold and strange. I left that night with a little hope, but really felt no better. It was the beginning of my recovery journey.

I began to follow a fairly traditional path to get better. My attendance at that NA meeting had offered some small measure of hope but I still felt terrible, and my family was overly concerned. They found a way to get me into a 28-day inpatient treatment program even though I had not used anything for four days, I went into their detox program for a couple of miserable days before I was transferred into the residential recovery program. I had been given a Big Book of Alcoholics Anonymous and been told it works if you work it. I found out there was a position called cottage chairman which I immediately aspired to attain. I started working the program, trying to fit in and wanting to be good enough to be chairman of the unit. Even though I still felt terrible, I had a new plan that I had not had before. I knew how to comply, do a workbook and look like the best. After the first week, I asked my family to bring me some starched white shirts so that I could look better in group therapy. I was motivated to do something different as a solution.

## Life on Life's Terms

After 28 days, I graduated from the program, with an aftercare plan that included going to 12-step meetings (90 in 90), get a sponsor, work the steps, and go to aftercare meetings. I had discovered that after a year of sobriety there was a way to train as a volunteer helper in the aftercare program of my treatment facility. That meant there would be a new position to work towards. I followed the plan and tried to look good while I was doing it. I did get a sponsor, and worked steps, although now I would say not very well. But I did want to follow the new plan, because it was the only other plan I had for living.

I began to sponsor people in the 12-step programs. I did take the volunteer facilitator training after one year, became a trusted servant in the program, and tried to start giving back. Even though I have been through many twists and turns, I have been continuously abstinent from all mood-altering substances since January 17, 1990. I went back to school and got a Master's degree in Social Work. I have been working in recovery almost since the beginning of my own recovery.

Only much later in my own recovery process did I begin to realize my problems had just begun when I stopped using mood-altering substances. The only issues that were resolved immediately were those that had been directly caused by using. Many other problems remained, with more life issues and problems to come. I didn't realize I was not well equipped to grow up and cope with my own life, so I made many mistakes and caused problems for myself and others. Learning to move through problems, changes and stress proved more difficult than I had imagined.

## Reality

All of this makes my case study, and Pam's, an outlier in outcome research, not an accurate model for recovery. That means we are not the example of how to recover but a couple of examples of the many possibilities of recovering.

As I began to work with others, I essentially tried to get them to do what I did.

I believed that if you did not get better, it was because you were not ready or had not hit bottom and/or were unwilling to do whatever it takes to get better.

I now believe that I was wrong. I am grateful for sobriety and my life now, but wish my own recovery had been different. I now know most people do not get better the way I, nor Pam have done it.

*Pam and Steve Moore*

# Ready Able and Willing (RAW)

*So we have to be ready, willing, and able to really transform ourselves, and each other in the world, not just say it and affirm it, "Oh, I want to change". Intention is important, but so is action.*

*Surya Das*

## How to Get RAW

### On readiness and the use of leverage:

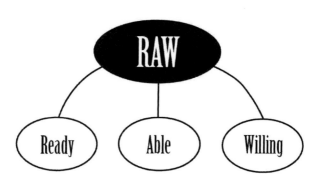

# Why Ready, Able and Willing Matters

The one parallel in both of our stories is that by the time we both got sober we were both, at least to some extent, ready, willing and able. Without a sufficient quantity of all three, it is very difficult for anyone to get better. Much of what happens in treatment for SUD is the push to help a person achieve enough willingness without much focus on readiness or ability. Without readiness a person will not have the willingness to do the hard work that is usually required to get better. We must also remember not everyone is currently able to get sober. Sometimes a person actually is not able due to their life circumstances such as finances and personal resources. There can also be significant mental health or physical problems which restrict ability to get significantly better.

If a person is completely ready, willing and able to change, they will be in the best position to use interventions and treatments to get better. We guess that is why, as treatment professionals, we prefer to encounter people who happen to seem most ready. Usually, they are at some crisis point. They are likely to be motivated to work hard and willing to go to any lengths to get better. At that point, a person will only need new information in the form of education, perhaps detox and then guidance and support for recovery-based life changes. Intervention and professional treatment are required when a person is not yet ready, able or willing. We must work with people where they are in the process, enable them to get ready for change without the use of leverage of forced activity or the need to hit a new bottom. This sometimes involves working with a person while they attempt continued use despite negative consequences. There must be a willingness on the professional's part to listen to failure and sometimes success of continued use while deciding what the success plan for recovery is going to look like.

***Telling a person to do whatever it takes (willingness) when they are not yet able or ready is worse than useless. It sets them up to fail.***

It is often easy to see that someone needs help. However, their need for help and our ability to see that particular person's need do not determine the likelihood of a successful intervention. Instead, we need to know how RAW (ready, able and willing) the person is. It is quite possible to be both ready and willing, but not able. It is also possible to be ready and able, but not willing; and we see many people who are willing and able, but not ready. We can successfully work with each of these circumstances if we are able to accurately assess the true situation. Probably the most used and least successful plan is to use leverage, such as force, to avoid the disaster of hitting bottom.

"We have to get him some help," says the desperate parent during our initial phone consultation. We can hear the fear and share the concern after hearing some of the details including a recent second arrest and persistent negative consequences around using drugs and alcohol. "He's going to kill himself or someone else," the parent says as we agree to see the person to assess and make recommendations. "I don't know if he will come but we are going to try to force him because he has to get some help."

The family is usually more ready and willing than the person with SUDs. It can be difficult to watch a person self-destruct that has no insight into what is causing their problems. Therefore, leverage appears so appealing to both families and professionals.

# Ready

## Working with Someone During the "Get Ready" Phase

We can often know a person needs help long before they are ready for help. We call this the "get ready" phase of the recovery process. This is also sometimes called precontemplation, the field research phase according to many models for recovery. One way this may happen is because of their age. When you are 17 or 18-years-old, it can be difficult to get ready when your peer group is using just as much as you are.

Dylan was 18 years old. He had been in a motor vehicle accident while drinking when he was sixteen and the other driver was killed in the accident. Dylan was upset and not equipped to handle what had happened. He began using heroin almost every day while still in high school. Dylan overdosed on heroin and had to be revived by paramedics on several different occasions within a six-month period. For Dylan, like many of us, using was a solution for his problem. He could not really contemplate a life without the relief of using. He was not ready, and he really believed that he was too young to get sober. His struggle was just beginning. While he clearly needed help and his parents were willing to pay for him to get it, he was not yet ready.

## Get Ready

The precontemplation or "get ready" phase of the recovery process is especially important and quite misunderstood. During this phase, the person knows they have a problem or problems, yet they still see the use of mood-altering substances as a solution. If we intervene at this point by simply trying to get them to stop using and get sober, then all we are really doing is asking them to give up their solution. In the get ready phase, the person is still trying to discover a way to make the solution of using drugs or alcohol work for them. Everyone is trying to get the positive results from using without any negative consequences. To the extent that still seems possible, the person will likely continue to try to make it work.

Sometimes the purpose of treatment is to work with a person while they learn this lesson. Rather than discharging a person that uses for non-compliance we have learned to facilitate getting ready by looking at what part of the use works, and what part did not work, in a way that does not convey failure or judgment. Treatment can help a person see the blind spots they do not see regarding their solution of using drugs or alcohol, and thus assist a person into a commitment to change.

Another issue that prevents a person from getting ready can be, because on the outside, a person's life can look very functional. They can go to work every day providing for their family, while the people around them do not have any idea of how much they are drinking or using. But on the inside, something starts to happen. There is discontent and sorrow that only they know. Most people usually walk in the door with a different complaint other than alcohol/drugs. It could be unhappiness in their marriage, job, or life. While assessing this person we can know rather quickly that the problem is how much they are drinking, but they will see the drinking as the only thing working in their life. In "get ready" we work with them where they are on the problem they have come in for, while gently nudging them to make the connection that drinking is creating many of the problems and distance between them and their satisfaction in relationships at home or work. What once seemed like a solution has now become a problem, which is a difficult, painful, and sometimes exceptionally long transition.

Pam worked with Jeff for two years while he was getting ready. He believed his problem was an overbearing girlfriend. He would drink to escape her control, often going home with a woman he met at the bar, and this in turn would create more distance and discontentment in the relationship as well as self- loathing. Pam was curious with him about the fact it appeared that everything he regretted doing, happened while drinking. Not only that, but the more he drank the more he disliked his girlfriend. Pam would sometimes suggest a plan of not drinking for a period of time to see if the two (drinking and actions that were later re-gretted) were related. Jeff would comply and have short periods of not drinking where things got better with his girlfriend. When the relationship got better, he would resume drinking and then the cycle would happen all over again. It took two years in the get ready process for it to click that the problem could be related to drinking. When the light bulb went off for him, willing and able came quickly. The recovery realization came, but Jeff still had much work to do. The recovery process can be very difficult but without force, leverage or serious consequences, Jeff got ready.

# John

John is eighteen years old and has been using heroin for six months. He has had to be revived from dangerous drug overdoses on two separate occasions. He still has his looks, a healthy body, is doing well in school and has no legal issues. Those around him are rightfully concerned about the two instances where he had to be revived but he can barely remember them. Because of the short duration of his use, he is not ready for help yet. He still sees both instances of near death as just bad luck.

Not all "get ready" issues are related to a person understanding that they have a substance abuse problem. Even in the case mentioned above, what the person realized about their drinking is that when drinking, they do things they regret. Their belief was that if they could better control the drinking, they would be able to drink without the consequences. That gives us a place to work. It does not matter if they say they are an alcoholic, what matters is the motivation to stop hurting themselves and to see they need a different solution.

# Able (Not Everyone is Able to Get Sober)

## Ability

The second requirement for change and the potential for recovery is the ability to do the work. There are people who have been so damaged by SUDS they are not physically able to do much work. They have developed so many physical problems from brain atrophy to late-stage cirrhosis to any number of other physical issues that they are not able to get sober. It is a difficult fact to face and luckily it is not very often you run into this, but it does happen.

Pam worked at a state-funded treatment program early in her career and an alcoholic with late-stage cirrhosis came in at the insistence of his family. He was a kind soul with a good heart, but only stayed for a couple of weeks. He came to Pam and told her he could not stay and he was leaving. Knowing he would not live if he left, Pam begged him to stay and told him he would die if he left. He knew he was going to die anyway, and what he told her has stuck with her for all these years. He said "If you are going to do this for a living you have to learn some of us are going to die. There is nothing you can do to stop it." He left and died two days later. That hard lesson was heard and remembered. Because of all the chaos around addiction it is easy to forget that there are some who are so far into their addiction they are unable to do the work to get sober even if they are ready. Perhaps we can find a way to be more compassionate with those who are unable.

It is fortunate that true inability is rare. In most cases, the inability is temporary and/or repairable. That means we must enable the person to get better by helping to discover the disability that is blocking them. We must assess and work with both the ability and inability of each individual.

# Other Blocks

Some pre-existing mental health issues make it difficult to receive the help a person with SUDs needs. There are times the family intervenes due to a dysfunctional family system. The family system is built in the chaos of SUD so they unconsciously block or thwart the person from receiving the help they need. At times there are family obligations which prevent a person from being able to get the help they need. They literally can not take the time from work without the effects putting them or their family in jeopardy of homelessness. There is limited treatment available to persons so there are times when a person is ready and willing but there is not an option of a facility for them to go to. Getting better takes much longer than we would prefer. One reason the 28-day model was so attractive was that treatment could be seen as relatively short term, followed by aftercare.

A major block for us to address is finding or taking the time for a person to heal and really change, and to grow. It takes time to get better. Usually, weeks if not months of regular work and contact with someone is required. At best, a four-to-six-week treatment model is time enough for assessment but not treatment. For years we have known that stabilization in a recovery process takes approximately two years. That is because we know the resumption of using rate is extremely high during the first 18 to 24 months after any inpatient or outpatient treatment process. Our treatment models should be based on two years not 28 days or four to six weeks. People often say treatment for that long is impractical but that does not change the reality of the situation. We heal or get better the way we do, not the way that is convenient, reimbursable by insurance or just because it is the traditional way.

Thus, treatment is an ongoing process. And during the early period of recovery you can expect some significant symptoms that need to be planned and prepared for to successfully navigate.

## Willing - Once They are Ready for Help, They Must be Willing to Do the Work

Recovery is hard work. Inside the 12-step community there is talk about the inspiration of desperation. In other words, once a person is ready to get sober there must be a willingness to do the hard work. Pam realized she was an alcoholic and had some readiness - the knowledge was there but she did not have the willingness. She instead looked for an easier way than the hard work required for sobriety. She went to a minister and asked him to lay hands on her to heal her from addiction. He told her it did not work like that and explained the hard work involved. She decided she was not willing to do the work involved and left. She continued on a path of destruction for four more years. She accepted she was ready and was truly addicted. It took more time for the willingness to be ready for the difficult work of change.

## Pain Is Part of The Process

To become willing usually involves some degree of pain. There is no reason to change anything that is "working for us." The theory of tough love comes from this line of thinking. It is believed that if we allow or cause enough pain for someone we love, we can help get them sober faster. Over the years we have not seen tough love help very much as it focuses too much on the relationship. When it comes to a family and how to get a person to see the best advice, we have to do the thing that helps you, as the family member, sleep better tonight. The best a family can do is begin to focus on themselves and helping themselves is the right answer. Unfortunately, we give family members a very mixed message about what would be most helpful to a person with SUDS. In family support groups, the loved ones are often taught something that is called the "3 Cs." They are told you did not CAUSE it. You can not CONTROL it. You can not CURE it. They are then directed to work on themselves and to get better through the healing process. This is probably the best and most unheeded advice. For obvious reasons it seems the person with SUDS is the issue here. To confuse the matter after being told they do not have any control, they are told not to enable, to support recovery financially and stay out of it. They are told if they do not follow this part correctly, the person with SUDS will not get better, and that they are responsible for the outcome. It is no wonder family members end up so confused.

Years ago, a gentleman came to see Steve about his adult son's heroin addiction. Pam and Steve were both into tough love as we had been taught, therefore Steve told him to kick his son out of the house so the user could experience pain and maybe get help. The father was unable to do this. Two weeks later, the son died of an overdose in the bathroom of his home. This father was wracked with guilt because he did not do as advised. At that moment, Steve thought, never again. It was not the father's fault his son died. His son died because he overdosed. His son could have just as easily overdosed on the streets as in the bathroom. We realized that we must all be aware of what we are willing to do and follow our own internal guidelines just as a person with addiction must be aware of their own willingness.

## The Right Way in the Right Amounts

It is often much easier to see that a person needs help than it is to figure out exactly what might be helpful. We often see some form of treatment undertaken at the point that the family or an employer or law enforcement sees that there is indeed a problem. However, many times, the person themselves is not ready, able or willing. If a person is still in the powerful grip of the belief that using substances is a solution and not a problem, there is almost no way to cause them to be continuously abstinent as a part of a new answer. Yet that is often what we try to do anyway because we can see abstinence as the answer. Some say treatment is easy. An old saying tells us, "That which causes a problem is a problem. So, if using is causing a problem, just stop." When we apply this simple thinking, it causes us to wait until problems get bad enough to hit bottom. We need new interventions that have less than simple solutions. To paraphrase an old saying, "Treatment is easy. But to treat the right way, in the right amounts at the right time, that is hard." All treatment intervention must first be based on the accurate assessment of readiness, ability and willingness. Getting RAW is most important.

Assuming a person is ready, able and willing, now what should they do? How long should treatment be and what form should it take? Over time there has developed a standard model of treatment that was based more on tradition than good outcome research. The model uses western medical concepts of admission and discharge to either inpatient or outpatient treatment. This model assumes that one can be quickly assessed and diagnosed. It also assumes that treatment is relatively short followed by what is called aftercare as stated earlier. This model has been a dismal failure in terms of outcomes and yet it persists in almost all areas of SUDs treatment. Assessment, understanding and especially agreement take a long time.

When a person encounters a SUDs professional, they have already been working on the problem and they have been treating it in their own way, which is similar to other human conditions. We try to figure it out and get better by ourselves at home before we go and see a professional. Therefore, diagnosis and treatment has already begun. No one has thought more about what is wrong with a person than the individual with a problem. We must hear that work and honor the process because it is a part of their recovery. This makes the ideas of admission, discharge and aftercare problematic and maybe self-defeating. When the professional meets the person with the problem, they are already working on themselves. We, as professionals, will join in and participate in that process for a while. When we leave, they will still be working on it. Thus, treatment is an ongoing process. And during that early period, they can expect some significant symptoms that we can, and will, plan for.

*Pam and Steve Moore*

# The Limits of Labels and Models

*Don't limit yourself to models and theories. They are merely tools to get you on your way. Consider multiple approaches. Be open to new and innovative ideas.*

*Franz Villa*

When we have a commonly accepted label such as alcoholic or addict, it is too easy to achieve a cheap and misleading agreement about the nature of a problem. When we look at a situation and say, "You are an alcoholic," and the person agrees with us by saying "yes I am an alcoholic," it would seem we have an understanding about what the problem might be. However, we may have a completely different understanding about the meaning of the word "problem." Many professionals do not even agree on the meaning of this word. At best we might have a simple agreement that the problem is related to the use or misuse of alcohol, but this is most likely the extent of our true agreement. **True agreement may be the most important aspect of treatment.** What we believe makes a person be the way they are determines how we treat them. **What is needed most is a clear understanding of why a person continues to ingest mood-altering substances despite severe negative consequences or the threat of negative consequences. To the extent that we understand and agree, a treatment plan is more likely to be successful.**

# Addiction Is Complex

An example may be helpful, one interesting definition of addiction is, "Addiction is a complex, probably genetic, bio/psycho/social disease process with equally complex and multifactorial etiology." Said quickly, it sounds very impressive. However, there is much to argue about and definitions like this may make agreement more difficult. The arguments over the disease concept are as many as they are unhelpful. The disease concept is a model for recovery that states addiction is a disease or that a person is dis-ease (not at ease). The disease model states that addiction is strictly a brain disease that affects the way the brain operates with compulsion to use, compulsive behavior and intense cravings. It states this is mostly related to genetics.

Addiction is a treatable, chronic medical disease involving complex interactions among brain circuits, genetics, the environment, and an individual's life experiences. People with addiction use substances or engage in behaviors that become compulsive and often continue despite harmful consequences.

Prevention efforts and treatment approaches for addiction are generally as successful as those for other chronic diseases.

(American Society of Addictive Medicine Definition of the disease of addiction.)

One day we will have better answers about the genetics of this problem. Today, we can only say that it is a probable genetic predisposition and is likely a factor in the development of substance use disorder. Bio/psycho/social includes everything, so we are safe using it. It also makes the term overstated for agreement about what the actual problem is.

For many years, and for most treatment professionals, the process of recovery from SUD has been based on a model called the Jellinek Curve.

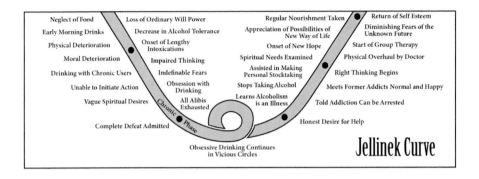

| Neglect of Food | Loss of Ordinary Will Power | Regular Nourishment Taken | Return of Self Esteem |
| Early Morning Drinks | Decrease in Alcohol Tolerance | Appreciation of Possibilities of New Way of Life | Diminishing Fears of the Unknown Future |
| Physical Deterioration | Onset of Lengthy Intoxications | Onset of New Hope | Start of Group Therapy |
| Moral Deterioration | Impaired Thinking | Spiritual Needs Examined | Physical Overhaul by Doctor |
| Drinking with Chronic Users | Indefinable Fears | Assisted in Making Personal Stocktaking | Right Thinking Begins |
| Unable to Initiate Action | Obsession with Drinking | Stops Taking Alcohol | Meets Former Addicts Normal and Happy |
| Vague Spiritual Desires | All Alibis Exhausted | Learns Alcoholism is an Illness | Told Addiction Can be Arrested |
| Complete Defeat Admitted | *Chronic Phase* | | Honest Desire for Help |
| | Obsessive Drinking Continues in Vicious Circles | **Jellinek Curve** | |

It is a neat and simple model which shows a downward slide toward hitting bottom from which point a person will then become willing enough to do the work that is necessary to get better. Once a person begins doing the work of recovery, the curve turns upward, and life begins to get better. The main problem with the model is almost no one's real life experience follows this model. And it has real implications for how we treat people. From this model we developed the idea that we must let people hit a bottom before they become treatable. The idea works so poorly in real life that we developed the notions of another bottom, the next bottom and the real bottom which became extensions of the same poor modeling. There is no bottom. There are only negative consequences that are sometimes severe enough to motivate temporarily, but rarely for long enough to create permanent change. Much of treatment has been based on modeling that does not reflect actual experience of either the problem or a solution. We need models that reflect the real-life experiences of people with SUD.

## What Is the MMRP©?

The Multi Modal Recovery Process© (MMRP) was developed at the Moore Institute and is based on our own research and experience. Over many years of working with people, we realized that in general we move too quickly during the treatment process. Almost every SUD treatment professional wishes the treatment process could be longer. We want a person to move from accepting their main problem is alcohol/drugs to working the 12-steps within a few short weeks in treatment.

People are often given a basic plan very quickly – Identify triggers, work the steps, and maybe a little trauma work thrown in there too. We see this model only working for the treatment provider. It became discouraging to watch the same pattern happen repeatedly. What developed was a black/white, pass/fail system, where a person would have severe negative consequences or hit bottom. They enter treatment and are asked to admit they are an alcoholic/addict. They see the other clients are following in this model and they comply. The problem is they are complying, but they do not necessarily agree, and do not necessarily believe their real problem. They might believe their problem is their wife being unreasonable, their parents harassing them and making a mountain out of a molehill, the court system forcing them, or any other issue except substance abuse.

In our private practice, people will come back from long term, very expensive treatment and one of the first things they will say is, "I am not really an alcoholic, I was just depressed," or something similar that indicates their lack of agreement. The way this happens is the treatment program deciding what the problem is without the client buying in and believing it. It is much more important to find some common ground regarding the problem. Agreement with the person about the exact nature of the problem is much more important than the admission of "I am an addict or alcoholic."

## The Trouble with Treatment

We are grateful for the caring treatment professionals who first helped us to get better and the ones that work so hard to help people with SUD get better every day. We acknowledge the sincere, caring people who work in treatment today. We know they want to help more people get better and are working within the framework they were taught, which many times helped them to recover from their own SUD.

As a part of our work, we have referred many individuals to inpatient treatment facilities. At one point in our careers, we were referring and following more than 50 people to inpatient treatment facilities annually. This gave us a unique opportunity to compare models, plans and outcomes. Although some things are slowly changing now, most inpatient treatment are still based on the admit, accept and comply models we have already discussed. As an exercise, we once showed our interns aftercare plans from multiple facilities around the United States. We used well-known places as well as more obscure ones. We used very expensive and very inexpensive programs, and with the letterheads concealed, our interns were unable to tell the difference. Discharge documents and plans looked almost exactly the same, and this was regardless of the client's circumstances. They were uniformly referred back for what works the best for most. Even more disconcerting was the number of times someone would return from a highly successful and well documented inpatient treatment stay, with a plan to try to be compliant but without any real agreement on the problem or the process.

## Randy's Story

Randy was referred to us after it was discovered he was using drugs on the job. A positive drug screen and his own self-reported using history were enough for a referral to an inpatient facility. He picked a good one and did well. His treatment reports were very good and included the often-used sentence, "patient readily admits he is an "addict." Randy's ongoing reports included terrific compliance with therapy processes and even a significant breakthrough on a childhood traumatic event that was to be followed in outpatient therapy. In our very first follow up appointment after discharge, he reported that he is "really not like those other people and the real problem is anxiety and depression." When asked about the report of his compliance, he said he wanted help and to do well in treatment and that was really the only way to get through. We started over and began the process of seeking real understanding and agreement about his problem.

## Both Addiction and Recovery are Conceptual Models Without Any Certain Meaning

There are multiple ways to think about and understand the problem, and multiple ways to get better.

Using the Multi Modal Recovery Process (MMRP)© we work with the client to discover how they are thinking about their own problem. Sometimes that might even mean assessing and redefining the problem as a client tries to find a way for substances to continue to be their solution for life (get ready). One of our most painful and difficult realizations is that most people use again. The truth is most clients drink or use then come into treatment and lie to the counselor and group about it. These clients keep any use a secret which prevents them from evaluating if their plan is actually working for them. Usually they will get caught, be given a second chance, and then be discharged or referred for more restrictive treatment when they use again.

We think there is a better way to work with them on being more honest about how their use went. Did they drink/use more than intended? Did they use only the substance they intended? How did they feel before, during and after? What were the beliefs they had about how their use would help them? Did that belief end up being true? What worked? What did not work? We decided it was better to use this field research in the treatment process and in the open to help with learning rather than in secret and having only their mind to evaluate the results with. That in turn helps lead to a re-evaluation of the problem and changes what happens next.

The Multi Modal Recovery Process© is based on each individual's current understanding of their own problem(s) and their unique and natural history of personal recovery, Therefore, it must be constantly evolving as new understanding emerges. This is based on assessment, agreement, and re-evaluation over time.

## The Multi Modal Recovery Process© Four Parts

The four parts of the Multi Modal Recovery Process© are:

# PAPA

## Problem
## Assessment
## Plan
## Accountability/Adjustment

## The Problem

No one thinks about the problem more than the person who has it. We respect that each individual has been working on their own problem for a long time. They have much time invested in trying to figure out two very important questions. "What is wrong with me?" and "What can I do to make it better?" Even when a person comes to us and says, "I don't think I have a problem," with a few questions and a little listening, we both quickly know better. What do not have is agreement or mutual understanding about the nature of that problem. All of us think about ourselves a lot. We try to figure it out and we try to make it better.

Despite some appearances, almost no one is actually trying to make their lives worse. We see that almost everyone we meet has been trying not to end up in front of a treatment professional. Nobody tries to end up seeking treatment for SUDs. We must respectfully listen to the results each individual has acquired from their own real world field research. How have they answered the question? Even if it seems wrong to us, we know they have a significant commitment to it.

In the following chapters we are going to look closely at each component of the MMRP and how it works. This will help all parties involved to be better able to see the problem and process in a way that is a workable agreement. This in turn makes solutions more viable, useful and attainable. It all begins with The Star Matrix Assessment System©.

# Are You an Addict?

*We are all different. Don't judge, understand instead.*

*Roy T. Bennett*

Do you admit you are an addict or alcoholic? Do you really accept that you are? These common questions may be some of the least helpful and most confusing that we have used and asked ourselves many times. We immediately run into the problem of the limits of labels wherein we can be sure we do not agree about what the words addict and alcoholic even mean. Then, because we have the illusion of agreement, we move forward to a plan for recovery with what is almost surely a basic disagreement about what is wrong. We know it has something to do with the use, misuse, overuse and abuse of mood-altering substances but not why. The old answers do not work. Why do I drink the way I do? Answer: Because I am alcoholic. How do I know I'm an alcoholic? Answer: Because I drink the way I do. Eventually we realized these simple answers will only work during a crisis and then only for a short time. We needed a deeper understanding and a more detailed model for the problems we are facing.

## Problems in the Field

As we worked in the field of recovery, we noticed that the question of whether you are an addict/alcoholic (or not) was limiting how we looked at the problem. We were much too "either/or" in our thinking process about the exact nature of the problem. People would often have the same diagnosis but different symptoms and issues and therefore needed different plans to address their problems. We wondered how we could measure what is essentially unique and individualized. With time and more information, we slowly developed The Star Matrix Assessment System to address the differences we were seeing.

The Star Matrix © is an assessment system based on the understanding that there is more than one path to substance use disorder and therefore more than one way to conceptualize the problem. There are multiple components which affect the most important question in all substance abuse disorders, the question is "why?" – why would a person continue to ingest mood-altering substances despite severe negative consequences or the threat of negative consequences? An assessment should answer that question considering all the possible factors which may be involved. There are five major domains research has identified as factors in the multifactorial etiology of substance use disorders that are commonly called alcoholism and addiction. They are:

- Genetic Predisposition and Biology
- Dependency (including frequency, intensity, duration and type of substance used)
- Co- Existing Mental Health Issues and Past Traumas
- Consequences (both from substance use, mental health and traumas in life)
- Physical Factors (including all other disorders, physical pain, diseases)

# STAR MATRIX

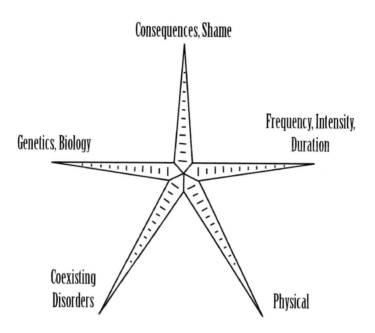

The Star Matrix Assessment System© considers all of these five domains and their relation and weight to one another for a more detailed and nuanced picture of the whole person's substance use disorder. The system utilizes both objective and subjective weights as the measure of each area. This is similar to a pain measurement scale, with the person deciding how important and how much this affects them and their life. We use a zero-to-ten-point scale with zero meaning no issues with that point on the matrix and ten being very affected by that issue. When looking at the above graph, zero is at the very center and ten is the outermost edge.

# Why It Matters

Our questions are too narrow. Is the person an addict or alcoholic? Do they have a Substance Use Disorder? These questions miss the ways each person is unique. Just saying a person is alcoholic or an addict does little to help us to understand what kind of Substance Disorder. For too long, a diagnosis of alcoholism, addiction and now Substance Use Disorder (SUD) has led to a standardized approach to treatment of planning without problem solving.

Unfortunately, sometimes this approach is not only unhelpful but can cause harm. A person will only comply long term with a treatment plan that they really believe in. What we believe makes a person be the way they are determines how we treat them and how they treat themselves. All factors must be considered. With the Star Matrix Assessment System © there is a way to consider factors and to help determine a plan with support and accountability that will work for that individual person. Using this system, we can look at the whole person and work with that individual to assess and come up with their individual and more natural plan of recovery.

We have been fortunate that persons enrolled in the Intensive group therapy process at The Moore Institute agreed to help us with our research for The Addiction Research Foundation. This allowed us to research, define and refine both The Star Matrix Assessment System© and The Multi Modal Recovery Process©. These case examples were persons who allowed us to use this information to help others. The names and identifying information were changed to protect their identities.

# Case Examples Using the Star Matrix Assessment System ©

## Connie

Connie is an attractive 66-year-old woman from the suburbs. She drank normally most of her life until her children grew up and left home. At the age of fifty she started drinking to excess. Since then, she has gotten multiple DUIs and created havoc in her home. She is well liked but when she drinks, she becomes angry and abusive. She has gone to multiple treatments and has attended AA meetings regularly. She has always kept a sponsor and worked the 12-steps multiple times. Yet she still can not stay sober. Looking closer at her history we find she was sexually abused by her uncle when she was 9 years old but was told not to let anyone know or "they will come take you away."

Connie learned to smile and ignore her personal pain at every family function. She met Sam, her husband of 50 years at a high school dance. They began an intense adolescent relationship and she quickly became pregnant. Connie was told that to remain a "nice girl" she needed to marry Sam and forget any dream of college and career. She became a perfect "soccer mom" attending every game, every school function for not only this child but the five that followed. When the last of these children left her home, she was left not only with a man she did not know but one she did not particularly like. He was cold, controlling and demanding. He cared little about her as a person but was concerned with the appearance of perfection as a family.

Connie was physically tired, empty and very lonely in her life. Alcohol made her forget these issues, so she drank . . . a lot. She would go to rehab and come home to the same environment. Her husband did not support her attempts at recovery. She would try to be a "good girl" and do the "right thing" and then spiral into loneliness and drink some more. It became a cycle. When she came into the

Intensive using the Star Matrix© we looked at their situation. She enjoyed the community in AA, so she kept that as part of her plan. She looked at the idea of divorce and decided that this late in her life felt like too much of a risk for her. She did allow herself to start taking classes at the community college that interested her, and she started her own business of an interior design company. She became more involved in her church.

She started to allow herself to know what she was experiencing and became more honest about her needs and desires. She learned to set boundaries with her husband which improved their relationship. She started exercising and eating a more balanced diet. It took all these components to improve her life and stop the cycle of relapses she was on. She thrived and learned she could handle both ups and downs in her life.

## CONNIE'S STAR MATRIX

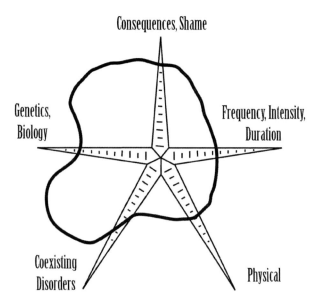

# Joe

Joe is a 28-year-old heroin addict. He began using at 17 and has been in and out of many SUD treatment facilities. He is from an upper middle-class family who has tried to help him in the only ways they knew how. They sent him to more treatment. Our Intensive group program, using the MMRP©, was his 13th rehab experience. He had an uncle who had died of alcohol related complications when he was young, so his parents were genuinely concerned and worried about him following the same path. When he was young, his parents were very involved in his life. He was bullied in elementary school but as he went into high school, he hit a growth spurt and became the star quarterback for his high school team. He was then more popular. He started drinking at age 15 just as his friends did, and they all drank to excess. College recruiters were scouting Joe, and he thought he was on top of the world. Then there was the car accident.

He was drinking one night and drove off an embankment and broke his back. He was in acute pain for a long time. He was bedridden for months. The doctors put him on a powerful narcotic in the hospital. It not only relieved his physical pain but his emotional pain as well. He would never be able to play football again but with the pain medication that did not seem to bother him so much. When he returned to school, people cared but not like they used to. There was a new star quarterback who was good. Joe started feeling excluded. The only time he felt any relief was when he took the pain pills, and so he started taking two instead of one.

This pattern escalated and the next thing he knew he was going to multiple doctors and getting more and more of the pain pills. Soon, the doctors started suspecting and said no more pain pills. Joe panicked and stole a prescription pad and wrote his own prescription for narcotics. He was arrested on his first attempt to pass a forged prescription. What followed was his first treatment experience. It was at a local adolescent unit for SUD treatment. There he learned about heroin.

It was cheap and easy to find. The first day of his discharge he found a dealer and began buying heroin.

By the next week, Joe was using intravenously (IV). He overdosed and had to be revived. He came to the Intensive after a relapse where he had remained abstinent for almost nine months. He was treatment wise when he came into the Intensive and knew what treatment professionals wanted him to say. It took a long time to get to the truth with him as he was very defensive.

Joe's plan began with the idea that since he started using so young, he could not really be an addict. He had attended NA on a regular basis and had "worked the steps" but felt they did not help him. He believed his problem was strictly because of the physical dependence – the injury he sustained in the automobile accident caused that. As we were able to look closer, he could see that before the accident he was drinking more than his friends. His family history was more strongly affected by the Genetics/Biology factors than he had realized. Speaking directly with his mother and father he discovered family secrets around other members who had died young of substance use.

With some time and guidance, Joe found meditation helped him with quieting his mind which helped him make better choices. He also discovered that due to the accident and subsequent drug use his maturation process was interrupted. Instead of a self-help group he joined a men's group that emphasized accountability and provided role modeling for him about how the masculine should interact in the world. He continued with in-depth therapy and found healthy ways of having fun and enjoying life. He recently married and is thriving without the use of any mood-altering substances.

## JOE'S STAR MATRIX

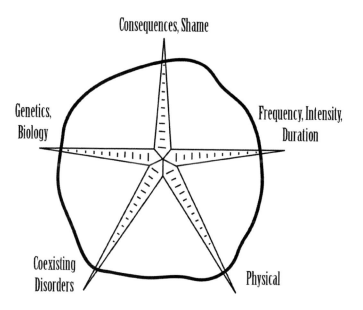

## Barry

Barry had been drinking a significant amount of alcohol for many years. He had lost jobs, relationships, had arrests for DUI and Public Intoxication with health issues probably related to alcohol consumption. When he tried to quit, he had withdrawal symptoms and returned to drinking even after extended periods of abstinence. Barry was raised by his single mother who drank too much. He never met his father. Barry was told his father had lots of anger issues when he drank.

Now at age 51, Barry reported that he started getting high when he was 15 years old and used lots of drugs throughout his college years. He always drank but rarely to excess until he stopped using other drugs after his marriage and began a career that required drug testing. His alcohol consumption and associated problems have steadily increased for the last 25 years.

One question Barry had never considered involved this: Since age 15 how many times have you gone seven days in a row without consuming any mood-altering substances? With some education and feedback, Barry began to realize that he had a long-standing dysfunctional relationship with mood-altering substances.

## BARRY'S STAR MATRIX

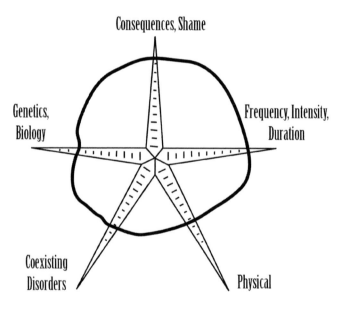

## Sam

Sam has been drinking a significant amount of alcohol daily for many years. He has had significant consequences including job loss and two arrests. His marriage was on the verge of ending. When he tried to stop drinking, he had withdrawal symptoms and always returned to drinking. Sam is 52 years old and reported he drank occasionally and socially until shortly after his 16-year-old daughter's death in a motor vehicle accident. He recalled that his mother died in a motor vehicle accident when he was 16 years old. Sam had significant trauma from both early childhood and as an adult that has affected him. He started using mood-altering substances to medicate himself. He realized he could not consume any mood-altering substances, including alcohol and heal. He needed to work specifically around trauma for his recovery plan.

### SAM'S STAR MATRIX

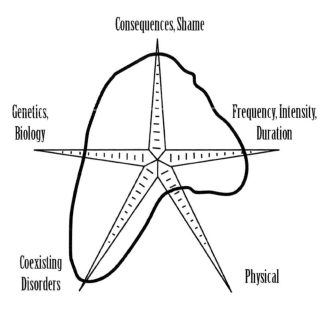

All of these people have substance use disorders that are most commonly called alcoholism or drug addiction. They all have presenting symptoms and problems that are similar. But they are not the same. The answer to the "why" question is very different for each of them. The Star Matrix Assessment System is able to help determine the difference and therefore begin a recovery process that is unique and individualized for each person.

In the next few chapters, we look more closely at the five components that make up the Star Matrix Assessment System and how it changes the way we look at both the addictive and recovery processes. With a new understanding and view of the problem of how people get better, we open up to the many more successful and natural paths of recovery.

# Genetics And Biology

*Genetics is about how information is stored and transmitted between generations.*

*John M Smith*

■

## STAR MATRIX

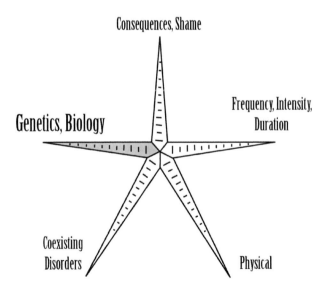

Consequences, Shame

Genetics, Biology

Frequency, Intensity, Duration

Coexisting Disorders

Physical

# Understanding the Biology of Substance Use Disorders

There is a considerable amount that we do not know about the brain and how genetics and physiology influence SUDs. One day we will be able to measure these factors more exactly. In the meantime, we must use the information we have, along with some imagination, to explore this important variable. We know that all people do not get the same effect from identical doses of the same drug. This can happen in two very important ways.

One factor is the subjective experience of euphoria. In short, some people like the way drugs make them feel more than others. We even believe euphoria may be a side effect that only a small percentage of the population can actually experience. Anyone could be temporarily affected by the use of mood-altering substances; anyone can experience intoxication, disinhibition and other common effects, but euphoria may be an effect of the few that we call "true responders." They do not simply get relief, they get true and complete relief. "I'm ok, you're ok, and everything is going to be ok."

Most people do not like the experience of becoming overly intoxicated. They experience it as an out of control feeling. A true responder never feels out of control. The more intoxicated they become, the more in control they feel. This is true euphoria. This is the experience we believe only some are predisposed to experience. This true response of euphoria may have a basis in the brain and could even be an inherited tendency.

# Stop Signal Vs. Go Signal

We also think some people respond to the effects of intoxication with a strong stop signal. They will begin to think this effect is too much and feel the need to slow down or stop. A true genetic responder never gets that signal. She gets the opposite signal. There is a strong "Go" or "More" signal that is always the response to any level of mood alteration.

Thus, what we think might be inherited is a predisposition toward a "Go" signal versus a "Stop" signal and a strongly reinforcing euphoria. The mistake we have made is to believe essentially all people respond the same to the ingestion of mood-altering substances and that most people are strong enough or smart enough to resist overusing. But what if this is not true? What if we are all responding in very different and genetically predisposed ways?

Early in our careers, one of the authors (Steve) worked with a particularly effective addiction medicine doctor who was not in recovery, and not personally experienced substance use disorder. Because she was a competent and caring physician, she would ask about his personal experiences with substances.

## Steve's Story About That Experience:

During one holiday season, we were chatting about going to holiday parties where alcohol would be served. I told her that I really didn't like to go to them anymore. I explained it was not so much about the temptation to drink but more about a dislike of the scene and atmosphere. The physician said something I have never forgotten. She said, "You know, I just don't understand it. If I'm at a party and I have that second drink, as soon as I start to feel it, I know I've got to stop." The moment she said that I knew I had never felt that before in my life. If I'm at a party and have that second drink, as soon as I feel it, I know I've got to go. I don't get a stop signal or maybe I should slow down signal. I get a let's GO signal. More is what I want.

As we continued our discussion, it became very clear we were having two fundamentally different experiences with the ingestion of the very same substance.

And as far as we both could remember, our responses had always been that way for each of us. This was something more basic than intoxication or disinhibition. At some level, she was getting a stop signal while I would get a very powerful go signal. This is one of the inherited predispositions to the ingestion of mood-altering substances. Some of us seem to have a big red stop button that responds to mood alteration. For others it seems to activate a big green go button.

Steve has told this story hundreds of times in many different settings. It is almost diagnostic to watch the audience to see whether the head nods at the stop button or the go button. Everyone usually knows which one they have.

Not long after that powerful conversation, a psychiatrist in the same University Hospital building was discussing euphoria as a side effect of some drugs. He said something important when he noted that pain or symptom relief was the goal of most drugs and that in some ways euphoria was an unwanted side effect that caused at least as many problems as it solved. In further discussions, and while evaluating research on the pain scales, we discovered that not everyone gets true euphoria from drugs and alcohol. In fact, most people don't. Everyone can get intoxicated and altered, but true euphoria seemed to be only for a relatively small subset that he started calling "true responders".

Therefore, someone who is most genetically or biologically predisposed to a substance use disorder would be a true responder to euphoria with a pure green go button in response to mood alteration. It is our belief that these factors can be inherited.

## Biology and Star Matrix

If these inherited predispositions existed, the questions must then focus on how to measure these factors. The easiest point to consider is the number of people in your biological family who also have some form of substance use disorder. We ask questions about parents, grandparents and others within the family. The total, and your direct relationship to the family members imply the possibility of heritability. Next, we consider the age that you began using and how quickly your relationship with the substance created any negative consequences. Finally, we ask about the initial response to mood-altering substances. This may be the most important, but difficult, factor to measure. Did you have a primarily euphoric response such as, now this is the answer for me, and I just want more?

With information about family (genogram) and recall of early use experiences we can establish a reasonable score for this area of the Star Matrix.

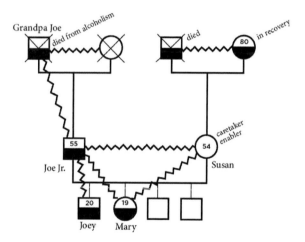

Genegram from Hellenic Family Therapy Website https://www.hellenictherapy.com

## Star Matrix and Genetics

There is a debate in the treatment field about whether addiction is genetic or learned. We believe the answer is most likely to include some of both. Usually, the greater the number of persons in a family with SUD, the more severe the use by the individual.

The other consideration on this point of the Star Matrix is whether a person feels euphoria upon first use as discussed previously. A "true responder" unlike a "pain avoidant" user will feel such a pleasant experience, starting with their first use, they can recall it with absolute clarity, while the experience of feeling normal becomes unusual. This increases the pain a "true responder" feels when they do not use a mood-altering substance.

## Meet Clyde and Debbie

To better understand the difference, let us look at the cases of Clyde and Debbie. Clyde comes from a long line of known alcoholics who were also functional at work and in society. He was a star baseball player in high school. Clyde was always well liked and popular with his peers. He had a 3.9 GPA. During his senior year he tore his rotator cuff. He required extensive surgery. He was given a powerful opioid narcotic for pain. With his first use, Clyde realized he felt a burst of energy and on top of the world every time he took one. He then realized two of these pills made him feel even better than one, but the feeling was temporary.

When this euphoric feeling was gone, it felt like his world had ended. He believed he couldn't manage life without the good feeling and energy he received from the pills. This thought turned into a belief that without the narcotic pills he was in too much physical pain to manage, which led to his cycle of SUDS.

In contrast, Debbie has been unable to find any evidence of addiction in her family. She was quiet and shy in school and a good "B" student. In the last year of college she was sexually assaulted at a party where she had been encouraged to drink. Debbie blamed herself and told herself that she should have known better. She lived in chronic shame from the experience. Her self-blame only increased her pain and the only relief Debbie felt was when she drank. The alcohol seemed to be a pain reliever. Debbie began a cycle of intermittent binge drinking when the pain of this trauma became too intense.

Both ended up with a cycle of addictive use, however both had a different physical response to the use. Both would be considered to have SUDS but only Clyde was a "true responder."

Thus, we could argue that Debbie was much less likely to have developed a Substance Use Disorder without the precipitating event (sexual assault) whereas, while Clyde was very likely to develop SUDs as soon as he was exposed to mood-altering substances. In Clyde's case, the injury was more a catalyst for what was going to happen. In Debbie's case, the pain (sexual assault) was more of a cause and effect. This distinction will become very important as we begin our plans to understand and facilitate a plan to get better.

### CLYDE & DEBBIE'S GENETIC/BIOLOGY STAR MATRIX POINTS

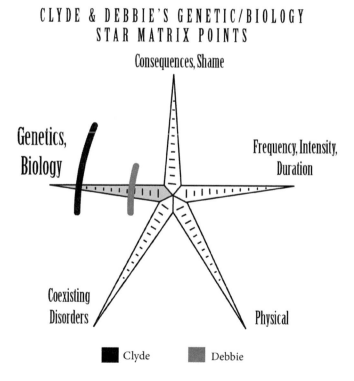

*Pam and Steve Moore*

# Frequency, Intensity, and Duration

*Life is not just the passing of time.*
*Life is a collection of experiences and their intensity.*

*Jim Rohn*

Another important factor in the Star Matrix is dependency which can be based on the factors of frequency, intensity and duration.

Mood-altering substances have known properties that include tolerance, dependency and withdrawal symptoms. The intensity of these is directly related to the length of time and the amount of substances a person has been using. For example, a relatively short period of marijuana use, even with severe negative consequences, would score very near zero (the center point of the Star Matrix), while a significant period of heavy alcohol use, even without any previous consequences, would be relatively higher. A long period of Benzodiazepine or heroin which are substances with high risk of producing tolerance and withdrawal, would always score near a 10 (the outer edge of the line).

The duration factor is directly related to the length of time and the amount of substances a person has been using over a period of time including a lifetime but most especially for the time that is identified as "disordered" using.

Other factors to consider are age of onset, gender, current age and complexity of the chemistry experiment (how many different substances were used and over what period of time). The earlier a person begins to use mood altering substances, the more likely there will be negative effects. Some substances (like alcohol) seem to affect women more negatively in physical ways. However, the more profound and difficult to measure are the effects of what we call "chemistry experiments."

When considering all of these factors, and when given enough information, we can arrive at a logical location for each person on the FID scale of the Star Matrix ©.

# STAR MATRIX

Consequences, Shame

Frequency, Intensity, Duration

Genetics, Biology

Coexisting Disorders

Physical

Therefore, it makes sense that if Clyde is using a powerful opioid narcotic every day and Debbie is binge drinking, his frequency would be more of an issue than Debbie's. Clyde will be more likely to need a medical detoxification program due to the number of times he has ingested his mood-altering substance, and it is also likely that he will have to manage additional long term physical symptoms as a part of his plan.

The last part of this puzzle is duration. In our previous example, Clyde started using in high school and Debbie as a young adult. Clyde's duration is longer than Debbie. In general, the longer time period a person has been using the more extensive the problem will be. Repeated exposure over time (duration) is what creates the primary effects of tolerance and withdrawal. Therefore, Clyde's FID would be considered to be a more important factor than for Debbie.

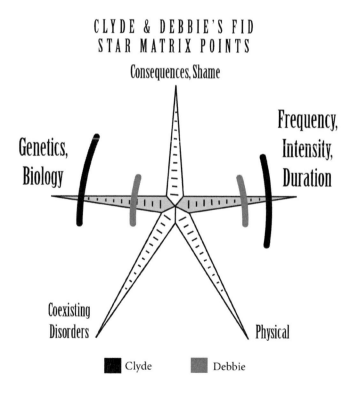

CLYDE & DEBBIE'S FID
STAR MATRIX POINTS

Consequences, Shame

Genetics, Biology

Frequency, Intensity, Duration

Coexisting Disorders

Physical

Clyde   Debbie

## John

John is eighteen years old and has been using heroin for six months. He had to be revived from dangerous drug overdoses on two separate occasions, but survived both times. He still has his looks, a healthy body, is doing well in school and has no legal issues. Those around him are rightfully concerned about the two instances where he had to be revived but he can barely remember them. Because of the short duration of his use, he is not "ready" for help yet. He still sees both instances of near death as just bad luck.

These Two Arms work together

# STAR MATRIX

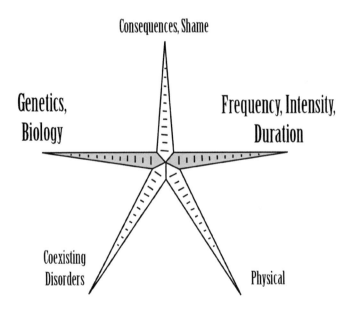

This arm of the Star Matrix sits opposite of the genetic arm and together they can be used to describe the severity of the problem with more accuracy. This can also show that substance use disorders which appear similar might be very different in nature. Someone with a very high genetic predisposition may have very little frequency, intensity and duration yet still be having many problems. While someone with a low predisposition will have more use over time before appearing as SUDs.

*Pam and Steve Moore*

# Co-Existing Disorders

*Working with people with co-existing mental health and addiction problems is one of the biggest challenges facing frontline mental health and addiction services . . . The co-occurrence of these problems adds complexity of assessment, case planning, treatment and recovery.*

*ALAC/MH Commission Report, 2008*

## STAR MATRIX

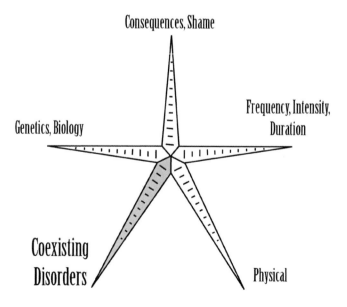

# Chicken or Egg?

It is well known that there is often a connection between co-occurring mental health disorders and substance abuse disorders. What is not always known is which came first. Did the mental health issue cause the substance abuse? Did the repeated use of substances cause another mental health issue that was not already there, or did the person have both all along?

All three things are true for some people. Substance abuse can mimic mental health issues at times. Sometimes a person is suffering from a mental health issue and they use mood-altering substances to self-medicate, while sometimes both are occurring at the same time. This makes the evaluation more complex but less important. Many people believe they have one issue that must be solved in order for the others to go away. Such as: "I have anxiety (and/or depression) and that is why I use." What must happen instead is that both issues must be addressed equally. Therefore, a successful treatment will correctly evaluate all issues with a plan to manage each, in the right amounts, and at the right times.

## Clyde And Debbie are Different in Some Ways

We evaluate Clyde and Debbie and their issues as both of their substance use progresses. Debbie had most likely developed Post Traumatic Stress Disorder (PTSD). Self-medicating with alcohol was the only way she could sleep without intrusive memories and nightmares returning. Her shame about drinking on that night, in addition to feeling responsible, kept her from seeking the emotional support and help she needed. Her drinking increased as she felt more and more anxiety and internal dysfunction from the untreated trauma of the sexual assault.

Clyde became increasingly arrogant and self-centered as his dependency on pain pills increased. The more he used, the more he believed he was smarter, more powerful and more able. He began to believe he had a specialness others do not possess. All of this is dependent on having enough pain pills. Even though this looks as if he is developing arrogance, this is actually an effect of the substances.

Debbie is relieving pain to function. Clyde has discovered a pill that makes him feel like superman if he can just get the dosage and quantity correct. Both Debbie and Clyde are having increasing problems in different ways and for different reasons.

Debbie's co-existing PTSD increases her score on her axis of The Star Matrix© while Clyde's resulting disorder moves him closer to the midpoint in this area.

CLYDE & DEBBIE'S CO-EXISTING
STAR MATRIX POINTS ADDED

Consequences, Shame

Frequency,
Intensity,
Duration

Genetics,
Biology

Coexisting
Disorders

Physical

■ Clyde          ■ Debbie

## Commonly Seen Together

There are many mental health issues that are commonly seen with SUDs such as depression, anxiety, personality disorders, delusional disorders and PTSD. It is difficult to tell if a person is suffering from mental health issues due to their use, or if they use substances to treat their mental health issue, or did they suffer from both simultaneously. This is why it is important to keep reassessing a person as they continue along the path to getting better. It is important to continue asking these questions over a period of time, which is one reason that treatment needs to be much longer than we might prefer.

When a person stops using substances as an answer or perceived solution to their problems, they are left with a problem with no immediate solution. The only problems that are solved by discontinuing the use of mood-altering substances are those that were directly caused by the use. In short, if I don't drink, I won't get drunk or get a DUI or any other associated problems. All other problems remain unresolved for a time, which includes all other mental health issues whether they came before, or after, the first use of the substance.

When a person stops using substances, typically they are going to be unhappy. They have often created much havoc and chaos in their lives as well as for those around them and it would be highly unusual if they were not unhappy. We are interested in whether it clears up with some stability, along with the person's ability to stop the dysfunctional behavior and learn new coping mechanisms. Initially it is very painful to wake up from a daze and realize they stole more than they thought, lost their job, or they really did cuss their aunt/spouse/parent/child and generally created heartache all around.

## Depression Or Heartache?

For Pam, heartache meant using huge quantities of substances, so she could avoid the grief from the loss of her two children. She had gotten arrested, been homeless, and had lied past the point of being believed. Pam had convinced her family and others she was dying of cancer when she was actually just trying to get people to leave her alone so she could use without being questioned. There was much pain that she had caused both from the worry that others had for her, and the pain of the lies. When Pam stopped using substances, she had to face and develop ways to deal with all of that pain.

For Steve, his problems were more performance anxiety and complicated grief. He had less obvious external problems. He appeared to be more functional in society but still had caused many problems and difficulties that he would need to address.

Negative problems that have built up for a person while using are especially hard because it is so depressing to think "I created all this pain all around me." Families are rightfully angry, and it can be helpful for a person to feel the situational unhappiness of looking at the harm they have caused. This helps them to emotionally mature, however, the more difficult part is to keep evaluating and examining the possibility that there is also clinical depression. There is a high correlation between addiction and depression, and there is still much to learn in this area. One area of research being conducted is the idea that, because an addicted person feels euphoria when using, living a chemical free life feels like depression.

Assessing other mental health issues that are associated with SUDS offers considerable implications for intervention and treatment planning. Some people may need to tolerate a period of feeling extremely bad, yet supported through that process. Others may require medication either near term or long term. That is why the assessment process needs to be unique, individualized and extend over a long period of time.

## Does Anxiety Cause the Problem?

Most people with any kind of substance use disorder report anxiety (or being stressed out). Many also believe that anxiety is at least part, if not all, of the reason to mood alter. It may be impossible to know which happens first. It is most likely that there is a different answer for different people. Regardless, many people who end up seeking treatment for a substance use disorder are very anxious.

Our experiences and research indicate that the questions are not so much of dual diagnosis, but the better question is, how much depression or how much anxiety is this person struggling with. There are many consequences from substance disorders and therefore there are many problems left unanswered when a person stops using. The question becomes, clinical or situational, rather than if a person has this issue. If a person is anxious, but they also have three DUIs pending it could be a situational problem, that will be straightened out with time. Likewise, there are people who have self-medicated their anxiety with substance abuse. If a person starts to sweat, have heart palpitations and move frequently in their seat, and it does not change even with time, this could lead a professional to start assessing for anxiety disorder rather than just being nervous. With each diagnostic situation the same thing would be coming up: is this situational or is this clinical, or both?

Cause and effect questions are profound in the area of personality disorders, and personality disorders are typically accompanied by three types of presentations: intense and unstable emotions, eccentric and odd behavior, or extreme fear or nervousness.

It is common for a person to take a diagnostic assessment when they arrive at a treatment program and score as a personality disorder but what is really happening is the person's impulsive and criminal behavior that comes with substance abuse. Since the effects of using drugs can consistently mimic a personality disorder, it is extremely important to provide enough time and effort to correctly assess before implementing a change plan.

## Sally

Sally was reported to be a "good girl" as a child. She was kind-hearted and generous. Then she began using opioids. As her SUDs progressed, she became more self-centered and would lie when the truth would have been easier. She started to shoplift for fun and seemed to always be splitting and pitting family members against one another. At the same time, she seemed very dramatic with her emotions and could flip from sad and depressed to a full-frontal rage within sixty seconds. She seemed to bounce from one intense love affair to another within a matter of days. Family members thought she was in love with the thought of falling in love, just not the commitment. People walked on eggshells around her afraid to set her off on another emotional rampage. While in treatment, she was diagnosed with Borderline Personality Disorder. As she became more stable in her recovery, most of the "Borderline issues" fell away. She worked, paid her bills, and met a man she related to and then committed to this man. Her mood swings leveled out which stopped her impulsive behavior. Her Substance Use Disorder was mimicking a personality disorder.

## The Good Old Days of Treatment?

When Pam and Steve first became sober more than thirty years ago, it was common to require a year to "wait and see" before a person was given a diagnosis of any co-occurring disorder to determine what would simply flatten out with time, and what was an actual clinical issue. There was value in that approach when considering that a person who could remain abstinent was given the time for a substance induced disorder to go away. People participating in 12-step recovery had received significant diagnoses such as Schizophrenia or Delusional Disorder, while the real issue was that the substances they were using created temporary psychosis. Both Pam and Steve experienced symptoms resembling mental health issues while under the influence of amphetamine like substances.

Steve was using cocaine and Pam with methamphetamine. Both are powerful stimulants that can have extremely negative side effects especially with long periods of use. Steve ended up in his bedroom with a shotgun pointed out the window after hearing people trying to break in, even though no one was ever there. Pam convinced several people to run and hide in the woods from the police who she thought had surrounded them with snipers. She finally convinced her friends to come out with their hands up and surrender, yet no one was there.

It would have been an easy assumption after either of these incidents to diagnose Pam and Steve with Schizophrenia, when in reality it was the chemical they were using. On the other hand, but much more rarely, we both have worked with clients who turned more and more psychotic as the alcohol was removed from their systems. The alcohol had a sedative and antipsychotic effect which prevented hallucinations and delusions. In both cases, the old method of waiting a year made issues get worse with time for some people.

## Sometimes Addiction Is Hiding Mental Health Issues

Early in Pam's career she helped facilitate a female factory worker's admission to treatment for alcoholism. The worker was drinking close to a bottle of rum a day, but the interesting part is she remained functional at work. Her referral was because she had friends who were concerned about her and how much she was drinking at night, which led to an intervention and Pam was called in to help get the worker into treatment. (At the time Pam's job was to work with postal workers during the treatment process – from getting into treatment, through treatment, and during the year following treatment.)

Once the female worker got into treatment, she was doing well until she called to tell Pam she had to hide a kitchen knife because there were people in the program trying to get her. Pam reassured her, called the staff at the facility to make sure they knew, and the situation was handled. The worker put the knife back and all seemed to be going well. Upon discharge she went into a halfway house for women. About two weeks in, the worker called Pam and told her she had to tell her the truth, that she was actually the incarnation of a new prophet. The next morning before there was time to intervene, she was naked, on top of a mountain of packages reciting long philological statements as she believed she was sent on a special mission that only she had the special powers to deliver. She ended up having to be committed to a psychiatric unit and began a long journey not of understanding substance abuse, but of schizophrenia. Her large alcohol consumption was medicating and treating her schizophrenia.

## And Sometimes It Looks Like Mental Health Issues When it is SUD

There are times SUD mimics other psychiatric disorders and there are times other psychiatric disorders mimic SUD, and then there are times when it is both. There has been a long and contentious debate over which comes first. It is our belief that there is not a simple answer to this debate. Everything that is debated in the psychiatric community is true some of the time. The same is true with the substance abuse community. **It is not helpful when we believe there is one clear and simple answer for all cases.**

# Post Traumatic Stress Disorder

Post Traumatic Stress Disorder (PTSD) is defined as: A psychological reaction that occurs after experiencing a traumatic event (combat, physical violence, accidents, childhood loss, or a natural disaster or any other event that creates a usually strong reaction) that is usually followed by depression, anxiety, flashbacks, recurrent nightmares, and avoidance of reminders of the event, according to the DSM-5.

As we have worked with people over the years one diagnosis stands out, PTSD can mimic addiction. A person will drink/use to excess, have worse or worsened interpersonal problems, and there is a clear escalation of symptoms. If you do not look at the precipitating events it would be easy to misdiagnose PTSD as addiction. After the Iraq war we often saw soldiers who would have a severe drinking problem. The interesting thing was that until their 2nd or 3rd tour of duty they drank normally and led somewhat typical lives.

Sometimes PTSD would occur from something they saw or witnessed and sometimes it would be from the normal trials of war, but something would change in them, and soldiers returned home as very troubled souls. The same would be true with sexual and physical trauma that happens to civilians. Trauma disorders seem to mimic substance abuse more than the other mental health diagnoses. The more trauma a person experiences the more multi-factored and difficult it is to treat that person. To make this even more complex is the fact that, as a person falls further and further into addictive use, the more trauma they bring upon themselves. People often believe they do not have the right to struggle with self-inflicted trauma, however, it is just as difficult as trauma from other areas of life.

## Clyde And Debbie and PTSD

Clyde, through his addiction, ends up having automobile accidents, getting into brutal fights and arguments with people and losing relationships that mean a great deal to him. All of these combined start creating a PTSD response in him. Even though all of his problems are self-inflicted, he becomes traumatized, and even though Clyde caused much of his trauma, it still caused a traumatic response in him.

Debbie on the other hand begins her addictive journey due to the trauma of sexual assault. When they both seek help, in some ways it is easier for Debbie because she points to the incident where she was a true victim and begins to recover. It is harder for Cylde since he was the instigator of trauma by his own

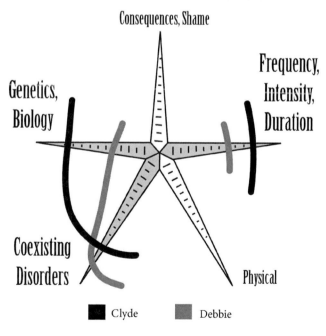

CLYDE & DEBBIE'S CO-EXISTING CHANGES
STAR MATRIX POINTS ADDED

actions. But Clyde's trauma is just as real as Debbie's. He has the shame (not toxic shame of self- blame in this case) of knowing that it is his own actions that caused his trauma. Sometimes it is more difficult for a person to own and work through trauma that seems to be of their own making. (This is where the consequences arm of the Star Matrix comes in.)

## Why Looking at Co-Occurring Disorders Is Important

The reason it is so important to look at co-occurring disorders is that for a person to be able to have a successful plan for recovery, all issues must also be addressed. It may be ill advisable to send a woman who has been sexually traumatized into a self-help meeting that is largely men. This may end up re-traumatizing her, therefore sometimes meetings that are women specific could be more appropriate. A person with severe depression or anxiety needs to be medicated and working with a psychiatrist and therapist, as well as, attending self-help meetings in order to recover. It is important that the whole of a person, all issues, be treated.

# Consequences and Shame

*Shame derives its power from being unspeakable.*

*Brene' Brown*

■

## STAR MATRIX
### Consequences, Shame

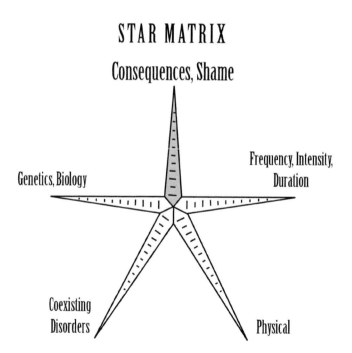

Shame is a physical, intellectual and emotional experience. Shame tends to be felt in the face (red faced) where a person will feel flushed down through the chest The chest will then have a tendency to tighten, and a person will have thoughts of regret and embarrassment for the event. A person can have healthy shame in the form of regret for violation of a moral code, whereas toxic shame is about the person believing something is wrong with them. Emotionally shame tends to be a blend of fear and sadness, and when shame becomes toxic or unhealthy a person will notice anger. Healthy shame can help to motivate change where toxic, unhealthy shame tends to keep a person stuck in their cycle.

## Consequences and Shame

Consequences do not affect us all at the same level or intensity. Often when we look at consequences, we want every adverse life event to affect us all at the same intensity and in the same ways, but they do not. There are people who can cause great harm and it does not bother them. There are other people who tell a "white lie" yet they can not sleep at night and they will feel great shame.

Two people are in similar motor vehicle accidents. One can have no noticeable effect and the other can not ride in an automobile for the next year. Similar trauma, external or internal, does not necessarily produce the same effect. In this way when looking at consequences we must evaluate the level of stress and shame an adverse event causes a person. It is usually the level of shame a person feels for an action that matters more than what the person has done.

## Help, Not Hurt

Toxic shame usually hurts rather than helps. Shame tells me I not only made a mistake, but I am a mistake. This is one of the many problems with shame. We feel not only the current shame, but the shame that is stored in our body from previous mistakes and old messages. Shame reinforces old messages we have in both the story behind the belief about our current situation and our "back in time" story. Shame goes hand in hand with substance use.

## Pam's Shame Experience

Pam has been pregnant twice. Her son was born when she was eighteen years old. His father was forty and a Vietnam veteran with PTSD. He did not want to have another child, as he had a son from his first marriage. They were not married. He had a propensity for violence, but she thought her love would heal him. When she was six months pregnant, he threw her around while yelling, "I am going to kill that little bastard." She knew something felt different that night. The next morning, he left angry. She did not feel right.

By the time the father of the unborn child came home late that afternoon, Pam was having severe labor pains. They rushed to the hospital, but it was too late. Her son ended up drowning in her blood in the birth canal. Pam was devastated. Her son's father was arrested for feticide the next week. He told her that if she would help him out and say he never touched her, they could be together forever and happy. So, on the day of his arraignment, that is exactly what she did. She went to court and said that she had made up what happened when her son died, and the case was dismissed. He laughed at her on the steps of the courthouse for ever thinking they would be together, and she never saw him again.

The shame and guilt Pam felt was enormous. She had no compassion for herself. She saw herself as defective beyond hope. She wanted to die. She used a steady supply of drugs and alcohol. Pam used to handle the shame she felt from the consequence of protecting the person who took her son's life. Until her next pregnancy.

This time, Pam was determined to have a healthy baby. She was not going to let this one die. She ate healthily, quit smoking, and quit drinking—she took very good care of her body. Pam was desperate for her second child to live. Once again, she went into labor at six and a half months pregnant, was given a C-section, and the baby was born alive. Pam was so happy, but afraid her daughter would die. She was very tiny.

As Pam laid in her hospital bed, she (not a religious person at all) prayed to God that she would give anything for her daughter to live. She instantly felt fear. Her mind told her that God did not love her, so Pam said another prayer that she would give her soul to the devil if her daughter would live.

Her mind had trapped her. There was no way out of this situation without emotional pain. Her very thought was that God was going to kill her child, since she had committed such a horrible sin. Within minutes, she received a call saying that her daughter was not going to make it. Pam was rolled into the intensive care unit in time for her daughter to turn her head and look at her, then the infant then breathed her last breath. Pam was burdened with shame and guilt. She believed that she had killed her daughter with her desperate thoughts. She was unable to forgive herself. It was a secret, and she began drinking daily to hide from the shame, pain, and guilt. This is toxic shame.

Every day Pam tortured herself with her guilty secret. As days turned into weeks and months, her mind started whispering to her that she had murdered her daughter. She was unable to look at herself in the mirror, and there was not a day without using alcohol or drugs because of her self-hatred. It is a huge consequence that using made worse. Her drug and alcohol use escalated until she became homeless. She was incapable of working. It took daily substance use to get through a day with shame and guilt. She remained in this trap until she found recovery.

It was a complicating factor in her addiction that had to be addressed to remain sober. By believing the thoughts that she could control her daughter's, son's, or her own fate, she made herself live in a personal hell. This in turn affected her addiction and chemical use. (Even though the deaths of her children were not directly related to her substance abuse, the shame and pain she felt after both died were related to using. She drank and used more to drown out the sorrow, shame and guilt.) This is how consequences and shame fed into her substance use but also were complicating factors of her recovery.

## Shame Grows in the Darkness

For reasons noted in Pam's experience, it is important to look at shame. Shame grows in the darkness of our secrets and the reason we stay in shame is because we believe we are flawed. The more flawed we feel, the more shame we feel. It becomes a vicious cycle that we must find our way out of in order to have a stable recovery. This is why community ends up being crucial for recovery, we need others to break our cycles. The first fixed false belief of Substance Use Disorder is that there is something wrong with me that only using can fix.

## Keep Assessing

There may be many reasons people are affected differently by shame and consequences. It is important to keep assessing for what the reasons are and then treat accordingly.

## Debbie And Clyde's Consequences

Let's look at Debbie and Clyde again. Clyde did develop some PTSD symptoms by the accidents and loss of relationships he experienced but he remained unbothered by knowing he stole his parents prized coin collection. He spent the money at face value on drugs even though the collection was worth tens of thousands of dollars. This was not an adverse life event for him before or after treatment, but it was a story his parents talked about that he found a little embarrassing but little other connection.

Debbie on the other hand felt deep shame about being late on a car payment. She believed she should, and would, be punished severely and that she deserved

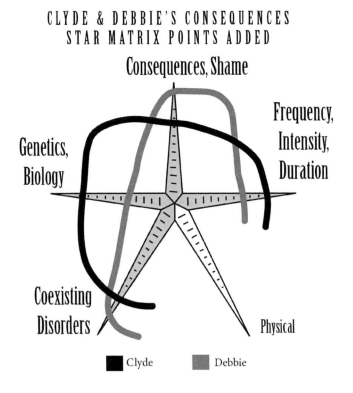

CLYDE & DEBBIE'S CONSEQUENCES
STAR MATRIX POINTS ADDED

Consequences, Shame

Frequency, Intensity, Duration

Genetics, Biology

Coexisting Disorders

Physical

■ Clyde    ■ Debbie

to have her credit destroyed even though she paid the payment and fee within fifteen days. To Debbie this adverse event was more severe than Clyde's theft of the coin collection was to him.

## Codependency Or Trauma

We believe that much of what we call codependency today is actually the trauma of living with active addiction (but that is for another book). It is our hope that a person is able to use the harm they caused, and the shame they feel around this, to help in the motivation for recovery. We have always disagreed with the idea that if you come to treatment for someone else it will never work. Sometimes the motivation of getting sober for someone you love does work. The shame of harm caused to others can be an excellent motivation for seeking help.

## Pain And Consequences

Pain and consequences also come from outside sources even before the first use. Growing up in a dysfunctional family has tremendous consequences for people. Janet Woititz developed thirteen consequences or signs from growing up in an alcoholic home. However, we have found these signs or consequences from growing up in any kind of dysfunction.

According to research by Janet Woititz, individuals growing up in dysfunctional situations . . .

1. Can only guess what normal behavior is

2. Have difficulty following a project from beginning to end

3.  Lie when it would be just as easy to tell the truth

4.  Judge themselves without mercy

5.  Have difficulty having fun

6.  Take themselves very seriously

7.  Have difficulty with intimate relationships

8.  Overreact to changes over which they have no control

9.  Constantly seek approval and affirmation

10. Usually feel they are different from other people

11. Are either super responsible or super irresponsible—there is no middle ground

12. Are extremely loyal, even in the face of evidence that the loyalty is undeserved

13. Are impulsive. They tend to lock themselves into a course of action without giving serious consideration to alternative behaviors or possible consequences. This impulsively leads to confusion, self-loathing and loss of control over their environment. In addition, they spend an excessive amount of energy cleaning up the mess.

# Adverse Childhood Experiences and More

A questionnaire developed by the CDC examines Adverse Childhood Experiences that would be included in the consequences portion of the Star Matrix. The questionnaire can be found in Appendix A, and this questionnaire includes questions about events that happened during childhood; specifically the first 18 years of life.

## From the CDC

Adverse Childhood Experiences (ACEs) are potentially traumatic events that occur in childhood. ACEs can include violence, abuse, and growing up in a family with mental health or substance use problems. Toxic stress from ACEs can change brain development and affect how the body responds to stress. Adverse childhood experiences, or ACEs, are potentially traumatic events that occur in childhood (0-17 years).

ACEs are linked to chronic health problems, mental illness, and substance misuse in adulthood. ACEs can also negatively impact education and job opportunities.

## How Big Is The Problem?

ACEs are common. About 61% of adults surveyed across 25 states reported that they had experienced at least one type of ACE, and nearly 17% reported they had experienced four or more types of ACEs.

# What Are the Consequences?

ACEs can have lasting, negative effects on health, well-being, and opportunity. These experiences can increase the risks of injury, sexually transmitted infections, maternal and child health problems, teen pregnancy, involvement in sex trafficking, along with a wide range of chronic diseases and leading causes of death such as cancer, diabetes, heart disease, and suicide.

Toxic stress from ACEs can change brain development and affect such things as attention, decision-making, learning, and response to stress.

Children growing up with toxic stress may have difficulty forming healthy and stable relationships. They may also have unstable work histories as adults and struggle with finances, jobs, and depression throughout life. These effects can be passed on to their own children. Some children may face further exposure to toxic stress from historical and ongoing traumas due to systemic racism or the impacts of poverty resulting from limited educational and economic opportunities.*

# There is More Than ACES

While working with clientele and looking at our own personal experiences, it is our belief that the list should be even longer and at times the consequences more severe than the ACEs scores. For example, Steve's mother was diagnosed with breast cancer when he was ten years old. For the next ten years their lives were a roller coaster ride of hope, then pain and dread as her cancer would go into remission and return until her death when he was twenty years old. While no one was at fault or blamed, this life event caused irreparable harm to him. He

---

* https://www.cdc.gov/violenceprevention/aces/fastfact.html?CDC_AA_refVal=https%3A%2F%2F-www.cdc.gov%2Fviolenceprevention%2Facestudy%2Ffastfact.html

suffered the consequence of cancer starting at age ten. The pain and consequences of losing someone who was there for him, loving and full of life, has effects for him to this day.

We have also seen that childhood bullying seems to have a lifelong consequence that begins before the first use. As shown in ACEs from the CDC, it is common for professionals to look at harm caused in the family situation, but we must also evaluate the consequences of harm caused by peers. We have found some of these pains to be much more impactful than anything inflicted by a family. People remain self conscious about their appearance, the way they run, they believe they are less intelligent, more of a nuisance than others, with all kinds of wounding from bullying. Anything that makes a person feel shame and less than others, or that leads to feeling guilt and remorse is a consequence.

*Pam and Steve Moore*

# CHAPTER 10

# Physical Issues:
## Disease, Accidents, Aging and Post Acute Withdrawal

*The wound is the place where the light enters you.*

*Rumi*

◼

## STAR MATRIX

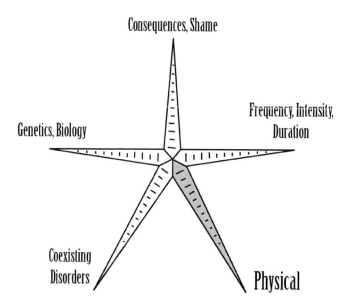

Consequences, Shame

Frequency, Intensity, Duration

Genetics, Biology

Coexisting Disorders

Physical

The last arm of the Star Matrix is Physical Issues. Like Mental health issues, physical problems could be masked by SUD, caused by SUD or both. Remember that the use of the substance is often a solution to a problem. This is true particularly in the area of physical pain and other discomforts whether they are real or perceived which includes physical ailments, accidents and aging as well as the severity of a person's Post Acute Withdrawal.

It makes sense that a person with chronic pain is going to have a harder time with abstinence than a person who is pain free. A person with chronic pain may use medications at times to manage pain. Due to having to use mood-altering medication, it is common for a person to end up abusing this medication. This is a common dilemma that usually requires the simultaneous management of two conditions.

## Post Acute Withdrawal - The Most Common Of Physical Issues

Terrance Gorski identified what he called Post Acute Withdrawal: Post-Acute Withdrawal Syndrome (also referred to as PAWS) is a cluster of symptoms that occur in recovering addicts and alcoholics. PAWS symptoms usually begin to occur between seven and fourteen days after the acute period of withdrawal, and usually peak between three and six months after the start of abstinence. The most common post-acute withdrawal symptoms are: • mood swings • anxiety • irritability • tiredness • variable energy • low enthusiasm • changing of concentration • disturbed sleep.

These symptoms may vary for each person in length of time and degree of severity and may at times be a hindrance for recovery. We have learned over the years that Post Acute Withdrawal (PAWs) must be monitored on an ongoing basis. A person will be active and engaged in their recovery but will suddenly be hit with PAWs and start to believe that is because of their involvement (or lack thereof) in their recovery process. This fixed false belief will then take hold and they become hopeless of getting better. They will believe they tried as hard as they could, yet it was not enough. The normalizing of what has happened to them is an important part of recovery.

## Chronic Pain and Recovery

Having been around recovery for a long time we have seen many people, due to having surgery or being in an accident, need pain medication they could not do without which leads to a severe relapse. In SUD treatment they are often not adequately helped with the guardrails they need, and it is a delicate balance to help them manage their pain and the genetic part of their addiction at the same time. It is not as if a person's body will know a "good reason" vs a "bad reason" if there is a genetic component to substance abuse disorder.

If a person is in chronic pain and in need of medication to manage that part of their issue, the idea that this person may abuse their medication occasionally might be the outcome and successful life management for them. "Progress, not perfection, does not equal permission" is the tightrope that must be walked. Ideally a person could return to abstinence and build a degree of safety for themselves without the shame they had somehow failed.

Medical conditions are a normal part of active use, and alcohol is the third leading cause of death in America according to the National Institute of Health.

An estimated 95,000 people (approximately 68,000 men and 27,000 women) die from alcohol-related causes annually, making alcohol the third-leading preventable cause of death in the United States. The first is tobacco, and the second is poor diet and physical inactivity. (National Institute of Health 2019)

Obviously it is not just alcohol that can wreak havoc on the body. Any chronic-long term use of a mood-altering substance is causing damage to the neurological system, the brain, organs and vascular system that must heal and recover as well. In early recovery the common issues we see include free floating anxiety, insomnia, stomach issues, skin irritations, and trouble concentrating (just to name a few).

## Clyde and Debbie and Physical Issues

Let's look again at Clyde and how the physical symptoms affect him. Clyde was involved in auto accidents that have caused chronic pain for him. Just because he has gotten sober, this does not take the pain away from him. In early recovery he

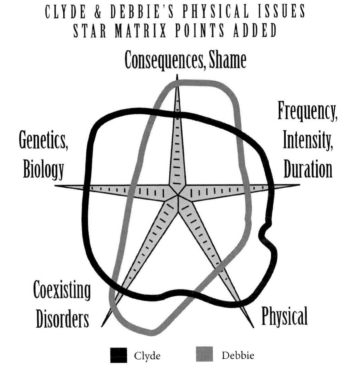

took opioids thinking that without them he would not be able to get sober, but taking the opioids triggered the genetics of addiction and he became a "chronic relapser." Without the opioids he was so distracted by the pain he could not focus on trying to recover. He can only be helped by thinking outside of the box of traditional recovery. His recovery involves walking a tightrope to shorten and minimize times of abusive use without complete abstinence.

However, Debbie's symptom is insomnia and the anxiety this creates for her. When she does sleep, she has disturbing dreams. She wakes up foggy-headed and tired, which in turn affects her ability to remain abstinent. Debbie's recovery in the physical area is more about managing the symptoms from PAWs.

*Pam and Steve Moore*

# CHAPTER 11

# The Plan:
## Possible Implications for Intervention, Treatments and Recovery

*Hope begins in the dark, the stubborn hope that if you just show up and*
*try to do the right thing, the dawn will come.*
*You wait and watch and work: You don't give up.*

*Anne Lamont*

### Back to the MMRP©

It is impossible to overstate the importance of agreement. For too long we have used a compliance-based model that fails to realize that the primary reason for a lack of compliance with any treatment plan is because we simply don't agree about what is actually wrong. Until, and unless, I agree with you about my problem, I won't agree with any treatment plan. Why would I? Why would you? We all do what we believe in. To the extent that I believe that you understand me and my problem, I will believe in what you plan to do about it. That is one of the reasons that our competing models and plans for recovery are detrimental to all the people who so desperately need to find a way to get better.

# Arguing Doesn't Work As a Plan

If you go to the hospital emergency room tomorrow for any reason and five guys in long white coats gather around you to argue about what is wrong and what to do about it, you are in trouble, and you would not feel confident about the plan. That is what often happens in addiction. Opinions vary. If you have a problem that involves the misuse or overuse of mood-altering substances, the plan for getting better depends largely on who you happen to see next.

If you are someone who has been traditionally trained in SUD you will likely be referred to 12-step programs and encouraged with the idea that all other symptoms and problems will get better over time as you work the program. If you see someone from traditional psychiatry, your use will be seen as a symptom of another primary mental state. The idea will be to fix your depression or anxiety so that you don't have to self-medicate with alcohol or other mood-altering substances. If you see a minister or other religious counselors, your condition will be seen as primarily spiritual in nature and this will be addressed so that the other problem gets better. Each of these approaches has validity and may well be the most appropriate in some cases. But how you are treated depends largely on the luck of the draw. Admittedly substance use disorder treatment is not the only place where this problem occurs in healthcare today. But it may be the most problematic. Remember, we are working with double mindedness and varying opinions about cause and effect.

The use of substances has been the most attractive solution for persons with SUD up until some negative consequences came along. For this reason we need a solution that has agreement and certainty. We have realized the limits of labels and expanded the model of addressing the problem. This implies that there must be more than one approach to the problem.

**In fact, we believe that there is a natural path of recovery that is unique**

to each individual situation. **For this reason we must be able to facilitate that particular recovery process, and we must be able to facilitate all forms of recovery with equal enthusiasm and expertise.**

Even though each plan must be highly individualized, there are some components that are consistent and will be a part of every plan.

## Our Beliefs are What Keep Us Stuck in Substance Use Disorders

A part of being able to address a person's Substance Use Disorder is to look at their beliefs. Our beliefs can help or hurt us. All people get stuck in their beliefs, but people who struggle with Substance Use Disorder, struggle more than most. The problem with beliefs is that we actually believe them. But how does this happen? It happens because when you add emotion and thought, and then reinforce this with more emotion and thought, a story is created. These stories turn into beliefs. When dealing with substance use, beliefs are of vital importance. These beliefs control how our recovery is going to go, or not go, on a daily basis.

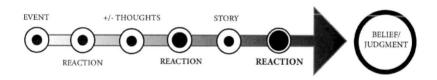

## Fixed False Beliefs

When we have a fixed false belief, we do not know it is fixed nor that it is false. We think it is the truth. We can know that an event happened a certain way, only to be slapped later with the reality that it was not at all the way we thought. And the more distressed we are, the more fixed the false beliefs become.

# The Most Profound Fixed False Belief

The most profound fixed false belief is that something is wrong with me and only mood-altering substances can fix it. When this is personal truth, it is easy to develop a belief that I am not the way I am supposed to be. If during early childhood, one experiences frequent correction of entirely appropriate behaviors, this can be translated into self-rejection. The belief that something is wrong with me.

In Steve's life, there has always been a very strong emphasis on religion and doing the right thing. Because he internalized a message that enough religious faith would banish all fear, that meant something must be wrong with him. No matter what he did or how hard he tried, he still felt afraid and angry, as well as bad and wrong. He made many efforts to change. Steve used his religious beliefs, dedicating his life to his religion and attending church more often. He believed it would relieve him of his desire to use drugs. It never worked for him. To this day, he is still often afraid, angry and sad because of his internalized message. He was, and is still sometimes convinced this means something is wrong with him or that he is not doing something right. This is true for him even though Steve now knows that his feelings are human and these emotions are normal. Still the nagging doubt occurred, and that is the nature of a fixed false belief.

When Steve discovered mood-altering substances in the form of his drug of choice, he found a way to make all those inappropriate negative emotions just go away. It seemed that he had discovered the answer for his flaw. Something was wrong with him and now it was not there anymore. What a powerful motivation. And every time thereafter that he used a substance to correct his perceived problem, he reinforced the belief. "Something is wrong with me, using a drug fixes that."

The way a fixed false belief develops is like this: Something happens — an accident, an unkind word from someone, we get sick, we fall down, we make a mistake, they make a mistake, there is an event — and we have an emotional reaction. The reaction is both physical and emotional in nature. Our mind does not process factually what happens; instead, it records the event as a threat or a pleasure. After our response, we have either a positive or a negative thought: "That worked." "That did not work." "That hurt." "That helped." "That did not help." "That was good." "That was bad." These thoughts create a deeper reaction, more intense feelings, due to the feeding of the thought and the first reaction. Then we make up a story about the event and reinforce our subsequent reactions and thoughts.

## Beliefs are Not Facts

Many of our beliefs end up not being true. The biggest struggle people seem to have is letting go of feeling like a victim, so they can honestly unhook from fixed false beliefs. The definition of "unhook" is to detach from or let go of a fixed thought, emotion, or belief. It is hard to let go. We use our beliefs to protect ourselves and our addiction. Substance Use Disorders keep us isolated with our beliefs so we do not have to look very closely at ourselves. Part of the work we do is to address these beliefs. Usually they are unthreaded one by one.

Only by being willing to take personal responsibility for ourselves and our lives can we grow. When we do take responsibility, we can grow by leaps and bounds. By owning the pain and paying attention to when we are reinjuring ourselves with our beliefs, we find relief from the need for a fix, especially a chemical fix.

## Family Has Fixed False Beliefs Too

In our work with parents of addicts, we see them fiercely living within their recurring fixed false beliefs. At the beginning of their adult children's addiction, they believed they could save them. Their children would tell them, "If you do this one time, then I will be better." By golly, for a day or two it would look like their efforts worked, whether it was time, money, or some other rescue. Then, after a day or two, the children would use again, and the pattern was repeated. By the time they come to see me, they have been in this pattern for years. Each rescue reinforces the belief that if they do "it" right, their child will be saved from certain death.

Parents always hear the stories of someone else's child who died. Because of these stories, parents feel they are truly fighting a life and death struggle. It adds urgency to the rescue that is difficult to see through. They are not codependent; they are heroic knights going to battle every day. Every day they end up with the reinforcement that they have kept this child alive by their efforts. And they wake up and fight the battle again, like good, noble knights, going off to save their beloved adult child from the dragon of addiction. They are blind to the reality that all their efforts are not working. A person with SUDS has to be Ready, Able and Willing.

We have a general policy that a parent (or spouse) of an addict should do whatever he or she needs to do to sleep better at night, but never with the idea that what they are doing is going to change the outcome of someone else's behavior. This is where the recurring belief begins. It starts with the belief that if I do this, it will change what you are going to do. It takes years to learn that there is only one person we are capable of changing, and that is ourselves.

## Effective Beliefs Are an Important Part of Recovery

A true or effective belief is a belief that helps a person. With the example above, it is easy to see that love is not going to heal another person who is not capable at that moment of receiving love. Hopefully, these parents will be able to see that love helped themselves through the hard times. This is an effective belief. I can not change another, but my love for others can help me through difficult times.

Another way of experiencing an effective belief is to believe that we can accomplish recovery, which helps propel us to do just that. We can not change or achieve any dream, hope, or desire for recovery without the belief that we can. It is paramount for us to hold onto these effective beliefs. They help us in our day-to-day lives to accomplish difficult tasks. And recovery is a difficult task.

## Ineffective Beliefs Lead Back to Using

A person's fixed false beliefs are what usually leads them back to using again. This is of vital importance to diligently examining specific fixed false beliefs that are always going on within a person. Just as an effective belief "I can handle whatever happens" is vital to recovery, a fixed false belief of any kind such as "I can't handle this," is a precursor to returning to use. Much of the work we do involves helping a person to separate from the inner voices so they can build an antidote to their fixed false beliefs. This is what much of treatment is spent doing. We can not work on the steps, on trauma, on mental health issues or all the many other worthy endeavors that are addressed in treatment, without working on the many angles of fixed false beliefs that a person will still have a difficult time not using.

The inner voices are going to distort and use the same methods used for recovery to convince a person to use again. People are told that they must hit bottom and do it for themselves or treatment won't work. We do not believe this. A person must be ready, able and willing as we discussed in the beginning of this book, but also a person must have the ability to separate themselves from their fixed false beliefs. This is accomplished through an uniquely individualized plan that is devised while they are in the first phase of their treatment and revised throughout the rest of their lives as they grow and change.

# Guardrails

In the beginning, no matter what path a person chooses for recovery, they need guardrails. Guardrails are protections we put in place to keep us from using. Steve was given an "allowance of five dollars a week." He could only replace money that he had receipts for. This guardrail kept him from having the money to buy alcohol or drugs. He needed this in the beginning. In early recovery there is a greater need for guardrails as a person has not experienced the confidence that they have the ability to not use. There needs to be protection built in. Sometimes this is hard on a person's ego and it takes some humility to accomplish this. It is hard for a person to admit they should not go into a bar or party alone. But sometimes they do need the guardrail of a trusted person with them during these situations. The more guardrails in place, the more ways that are implemented to keep a person from using in the beginning, the more likely there will be success. The more occasions that are met with success, the more confident a person becomes at believing they can be successful. For a person to find long term sobriety they must believe it is possible. The guardrails give them the protection to have the success they need. As time goes on and they become more stable in their recovery, the less need for guardrails there will be.

# Possible Guardrails

As a part of accountability, these are possibilities in the areas of money, time and effort:

- Let someone else control money and assets (don't carry cash).

- Volunteer to be randomly drug screened.

- Take a support person who understands your risks for drinking/using.

- Avoid time alone. Be in the company of others even when difficult.

- Read supporting literature.

- Meditate in some form daily.

- Attend self-help or other community support meetings.

- A peppermint (yes, sometimes sucking on a peppermint can lessen the desire to use).

- Stay accountable with a trusted person.

- Use prayer or other forms of consciousness.

- Incorporate affirmations and spirituality.

- Think it through - what would be lost with continued use.

## Distraction And Containment

Another important part of every plan is distraction and containment. A person can not work on themselves all of the time and they need a way to have healthy distraction. Sometimes even a distraction that other people see as unhealthy can help especially in the beginning. TV, reading, even shopping might work for a while. Healthier distractions might be hiking, meditation, organized sports, or rock climbing. Either way it is important for a person to know that any distraction that helps them through a craving is an asset.

Containment is what Pam did for her own recovery. She would not allow herself to go outside if she felt anxiety or a craving because she knew she would use it if she did. She contained herself during a craving. This built resilience. And with resilience comes more confidence, and as we discussed earlier, the more confident a person is that they can do what it takes to stay sober, the more likely they are to stay sober.

## Circles – A Way to Look at the Direction of the Arrow

Recovery is never a straight line. Instead, we need to be looking at the direction of the arrow. Is this person moving in a direction that is most likely to produce results which will lead to recovery or is this person doing things and moving in a direction that is most likely going to lead back to using. We measure this in a visual way with the recovery circles.

A person's plan is developed in three stages – what I am doing, what my life looks like when I am doing what works for me; what my life looks like and what I am doing when I am starting to believe things that are not true; and what relapse looks like for me. The circles model was adapted from the Sex Addicts Anonymous pamphlet entitled Three Circles.

Clyde's plan involved healthy features such as massage, meditation, physical therapy and seeing a reputable pain management professional that uses methods other than opioids (physical therapy, acupuncture, breath work, etc.), along with 12-step meeting attendance, prayer and meditation, using a sponsor to help him work the steps and exercise. He spends time with both friends that are in recovery and with his family. He knows that he starting to slip into the potential for relapse when he starts avoiding friends, family and his sponsor, stops going to meetings, and spends time dwelling on how unfair it is that he has to live with chronic pain.

He starts to believe the false belief that he can not handle the pain he is in. He knows he has "relapsed" when he starts adjusting his medication on his own, smoking pot (just for the pain) or drinking (just to help ease the pain and discomfort). The more aware he is when focusing on the healthy function, along with the fewer risky behaviors he does, the more likely he will be able to address his fixed false beliefs before he returns to substance abuse.

## CLYDE'S RECOVERY CIRCLES

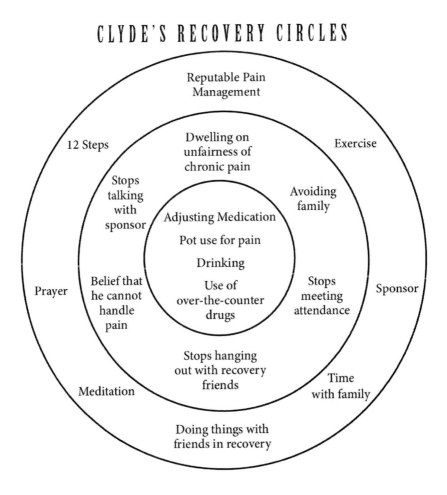

On the other hand, Debbie's plan for recovery involves going to both a trauma group and individual therapy; practicing daily self-care such as meditation and journaling; and taking time for fun play such as hiking and biking which she enjoys tremendously. Her recovery involves church attendance and being involved with a close circle of friends. She knows she is slipping when she starts to view herself as only a victim of her abuse and starts to isolate and believe that she will never be able to live down the trauma of her rape, that it has "ruined her

## DEBBIE'S RECOVERY CIRCLES

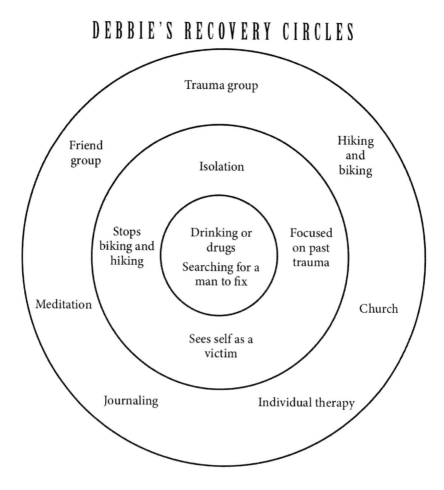

for life." She knows her arrow is going in the wrong direction when she avoids church and her friend circle, or when she stops doing activities she enjoys. Debbie knows she has relapsed when she drinks again or starts thinking she needs a man and believing she can fix him.

The plan must be individualized specifically for Clyde. Based on Clyde's Matrix, it is apparent that although he needs some accommodation for his chronic pain issues, he will easily fit into the traditional recovery plan of AA, sponsor and prayer and meditation. Because he is a true responder he will identify with the people within the "rooms." He did not have any trauma until his addiction and the accidents and AA has been effective in dealing with this type of trauma, so Clyde has a good chance of thriving within this program.

However, because of Debbie's early rape, the effects probably would not be a good fit for the traditional path of recovery. She needs a program that will address her trauma in a safe and nurturing way. She does not have a genetic link to addiction. Her substance use disorder began as a pain management technique, so her recovery needs to address her issues in a more private and intimate manner, and therefore, she will have better results in a closed group and individual therapy. Debbie needs to address her original pain with the idea that this will in turn address the need she had to self-medicate. Clyde and Debbie both have a need for abstinence but for very different reasons. This is why each plan should be unique and individualized for the person based on their Star Matrix Assessment. With the plan comes accountability and re-assessment of the plan.

*Pam and Steve Moore*

# CHAPTER 12

# Accountability/ Adjustment

*I have a plan of action, but the game is a game of adjustments.*

*Mike Krzyzewski*

It is easy to see that the plan has failed when disaster strikes. What we need is a way to see and adjust the plan based on early indicators that arise before disaster occurs.

In recovery there is a concept called the invisible line. No one would cross it if they could see it. The problem is that it is crossed before seen. There is no way to make an invisible line visible to me, but I can use all available information to know how best to avoid it all together.

One possible way is to have boundaries that are so firm that I can never even get close to any line. This can work but can also be problematic in terms of real life situations. Often it is recommended that people change their entire lives and get new friends and places to go ("change your playmates and playgrounds"). Sometimes this is more advisable than actually possible.

# Clay

Clay was a 48-year-old pharmacist who became addicted to narcotics taken from his job. While it is possible to change careers completely, it is not plausible, therefore Clay has had to learn to take extra care of himself to stay in his profession. He has built extra accountability into his plan for continued abstinence from mood-altering substances. In the beginning he requested this by asking his boss to have another person count the narcotics at the end of his shift to assure that none were missing and to prevent himself from slipping a little medication for himself.

# James

James is married to Kathy who still drinks alcohol socially. She has never had a problem and would prefer to continue to drink at times. As part of his plan, James and his wife must address how and when she will drink.

# Community

One of the main ways we develop our accountability is through community. The community could be the traditional AA community, but it could also be my church group, a yoga circle, a therapy group or therapist, a trusted mentor, family members or any other person or group that can be trusted to speak difficult truths when needed.

The reason a community is so important is that they can see the back of my head. In other words, because of fixed false beliefs and the role they play in returning to substance use, we need people in our lives who can help us see what we can not see on our own. Although Pam did not fit well in the AA paradigm, what she did have was a very trusted friend early during her recovery who cared enough to always tell Pam the truth about what he saw in her. He was quick to point out when she was saying or doing something that would harm herself, whether it was from self-victimization, to trying to fix herself through relationships or that she was going to risky places. Her community was small but it worked. Steve on the other hand thrived in the AA community and had both a sponsor and a "home group" that was quick to point out to him that he was falling back into old behaviors and beliefs. Pam's way would not have worked for Steve, nor Steve's way for Pam.

## Family is Community Too

Family can end up being an important part of the recovery process. At the same time they can also be part of the community that sabotages a person because of their own fears, traumas and beliefs from having been affected by substance abuse disorder with a person – effects will probably linger for the rest of their lives.

For the same reason a family can sabotage a person's recovery, they can also help. A family member has experienced the trauma and pain of a person's dysfunctional use. Due to this experience and the heartaches that have come from the use, they usually know with the smallest of details when a substance user is falling back into old beliefs. They know the smallest telltale sign(s). We have encouraged family members to help a person write their signs of growth and degeneration together at times when life is smooth.

Because the family sees what a person can not (the back of their head), they also have information about signs to look for better than anyone. The trick is to relay this information without thinking they need to micromanage it. It is a very thin line, but it is an important part of accountability that can be of huge benefit to a person's recovery process.

We personally do this for one another. Pam will tell Steve when she sees him slipping into his relapse behaviors and he does the same for her, and it has helped.

## Accountability and Adjustment

The self-help community – therapists, friends, mentors, wise elders, church members, yoga groups and others – are also important parts of accountability. Accountability for a person's relapse is too great of a burden for it to be left up just to family. There is so much fear for families, that carrying all of the accountability becomes destructive. The family members tend to become over responsible for their loved one's sobriety. Family members are so close and love so much they can start to see the person's recovery as their duty to ensure. Due to the nature and intimacy of these relationships, family should not be the sole accountability partner for a person, and while the family is important, they should not be the only source of accountability. Luckily, there are many options for people to choose from – the way we see it, it is more important that a person gets better rather than how they get better.

As a person moves along in their recovery, what they see as a return to addictive use changes. In the beginning, not using is the main focus of a person's plan for recovery. As a person matures in their recovery, what is dysfunctional becomes more important in their lives. Today one of Pam's relapses is when she gets lost in negative thinking along with beliefs that take away the tranquility of her life and those she loves. For Steve, one of his relapses is the return to the use of Tylenol. It affects the way he sees himself. Therefore, recognizing what a relapse looks like has grown for both of them. A plan is ever changing, so accountability must be ever changing also. What works for a person the first year will not work in year two. Likewise, what worked in year two will not work in year three, and so on. This will go on for the rest of our lives. We will always be evolving and changing. The plan changes.

Because the plan is always evolving, we can imagine a person saying I have been "in recovery" (from my SUDs) for the past 21 years, and I have been completely abstinent from all mood-altering substances for the last 14 years. We can understand why some might say this is an unnecessary expansion of the definition of recovery or even just a tricky semantic device. We think it is an important adjustment that allows people to pass more quickly into full recovery and getting better. This is because we stop failing them so much at the beginning of their process. It is more complex and difficult to work in the gray area, but it has the great benefit of reflecting most people's real-life experience.

Our book is meant to be suggestive only. We realize we know only a little. (Page 164, Big Book of Alcoholics Anonymous)

We have been extremely fortunate to work with many people who have gotten better. Our recurring motto has become – "We care very much that you get better. We don't care very much how."

With the last statement, everyone is relieved of the burden of certainty about what recovery should look like or how one should get there. The only thing that we are adamantly against is the continued suffering that comes from substance use disorders. To that end, we will walk your natural path of recovery. May we all find that now.

*Pam and Steve Moore*

# CHAPTER 13

# Success on the Natural Path

*If you find a path with no obstacles, it probably doesn't lead anywhere.*

*Frank A. Clark*

■

We wanted to end this book with examples of people who found their personal success on the natural path of recovery. It is a way to see how a person may take many roads to their success and we hope you can see that what is success for one person may be wrong for another. We appreciate not only these individuals but all those who have allowed us the honor of watching their personal journey on their path of recovery.

## Barbara

Barbara came in to see us as a 26-year-old woman struggling with alcohol use. She was physically sick from her alcohol consumption. She had the shakes and her blood pressure was high. Barbara was from a long line of alcoholics, and her mother had died three years before from alcoholism. She did not want to end up with the same result, so she was willing to begin treatment.

Her first task was to physically recuperate, and for this she went into a detox unit. Upon her return she was able to work on herself in our group. She drank again thirty-three days into her group process and stayed intoxicated for four days. Upon her return to the group she was ready for the difficult work of staying sober. Had it not been for the four days of drinking, Barbara would not have been ready for sobriety since she was not completely sure she could never drink again. The temporary use helped her to see that she had more than a push to stay sober, she also had a pull – she wanted to live a different kind of life than what she experienced growing up.

Barbara was a good fit for the Alcoholics Anonymous program and thrived both in the community of women she met there, and by working the 12-steps. She also began sponsoring and helping other women. At two years sober, she drank again for four days and hit a wall of despair that had its roots in her childhood. She quickly returned to meetings and began therapy to deal with the pain and loss of growing up in an alcoholic home. Due to her sobriety, she was able to go back to college and begin a career in finance, and there she met her husband. She currently has two children and is living a successful life. She remains in the 12-step program to this day.

## Adam

When Adam first came in for treatment he was very distraught because of the recent death of his sibling. They had been very close and long time drinking buddies. Most of their lives and activities had been based on consuming very large amounts of alcohol. To Adam that seemed normal. However, he knew that his sibling's death had been caused by drinking and he wanted to work on his own over-consumption. Despite the detrimental precipitating event, Adam was not ready to stop drinking. In fact, his first goal was to limit himself to 10 shots per day. This would actually be a reduction. He did not want to go to 12 Step meetings because of significant religious objections, so we began working to get ready for change starting exactly where he was.

We stayed connected to him and worked weekly in therapy to document the results of Adam's plan and help him get ready. We introduced SMART recovery concepts and tools, then we invited him to attend a meeting. He became involved and started working on the problem long before he achieved any abstinence. He overcame many difficulties and setbacks while staying connected to the process. Today, he is a trained volunteer facilitator for SMART meetings* and has maintained complete abstinence for over 3 years.

# Lee

Lee came in to see us for a drinking problem that no one knew about but him. He would hide in his "man cave" at night and drink. His wife knew he drank too much, but he was drinking three times more than she knew. He wanted to try and stay sober on his own without meetings or going into the Intensive group. He worked with Pam on some issues about fixed false beliefs. He believed his drinking gave him confidence and made him a better salesman, and he believed his wife's anger was about being unhappy with her own life, not that he spent so much time in his "man cave" and away from the family. He committed to stop drinking at his first session, and he worked on his fixed false beliefs in sessions. He worked on being kinder to his wife and spent time out of the basement and with his family. His family life greatly improved and he noticed his commissions grew as he could remember what had happened during his sales calls. It has been over two years since he walked into our door, and he has not returned to alcohol since. His plan involved internal changes that worked for him.

*Self-Management And Recovery Training (SMART) is a global community of mutual-support groups. At meetings, participants help one another resolve problems with any addiction. Contact information pg. 147.

# Frank

Frank had a long history of anger and acting out while intoxicated. He was young and worked in the restaurant business. He had been raised by a single mom who later became a counselor herself, so Frank had exposure to some concepts related to mental health and recovery issues. His initial exposure to 12-step meetings were coerced by mom and the court system. He had been forced into treatment and attending meetings many times in the past. When we first saw him, he was sure that his problem was a lack of compliance because he was stubborn and unwilling. After some intensive group work, he was able to deconstruct some of his previous beliefs about his problems, possible solutions, and to re-evaluate a path forward. Frank had an attraction to mediation practice and with a little encouragement he became involved in Recovery Dharma, a Buddhist-based path to getting better. He now has a successful career and family life that is based on abstinence and these principles.

# Leroy

Leroy had been in Narcotics Anonymous for fifteen years. He started in the 12-step programs when he was 17 years old. Leroy drank and did opioids from the time he was 14 years old, until his family intervened at age 17. He was active, but unhappy going to meetings and he was not sure he was a "true addict." Leroy worked on issues surrounding early trauma while he was with us, he did deep interpersonal work and felt clearer about himself and who he was. At this time, he decided he wanted to have a glass of wine with his dinner and gave himself the option to have up to three glasses of wine, no more than twice a week. He decided to quit Narcotics Anonymous and instead focus on his faith. He became very active in his church and assumed a position of leadership. He is now married and has two children. Ten years have passed and Leroy continues to limit his wine to three glasses, no more than twice a week. He is still very active in the leadership of his church and is married and raising healthy happy children. This is his path of recovery.

## Caroline

Caroline, a woman in her mid-fifties, had been drinking very heavily for the last 15 years of her adult life. Her family was very concerned for her health and well being because she lived alone and seemed to have few friends. Caroline did not want to stop drinking and had aversion to any type of religious organization. She worked on her family and relationship issues for many months in group therapy. During that time she reduced her alcohol consumption to ingesting two wine coolers per day. For the last five years, Caroline has maintained that level of consumption, as well as a new job along with some new outside interests. Both she and her family consider her treatment and outcome to be a great success. At last report she was happy and doing well.

## William

William came from a family with a history that was very significant for both alcoholism and suicide. When he began to have significant problems with his own drinking, William thought that he knew how to get it under control. He made many attempts on his own but each time he resumed drinking. He lost his job because of drinking and finally began the process of understanding his problem. With work in intensive group therapy, he began to see that his desire to please others and fit in was undermining his efforts to get better. He embarked on a one-year plan to fit into Alcoholics Anonymous and has been successful for the past few years.

# Burt

When Burt discovered heroin, he believed that he had finally found the answer for all his insecurities and fears. He tried for years to find a way to be a successful drug user and at times that seemed to be working for him. He had married and had a child while maintaining a successful business. But over time, his use had caught up with him and he eventually lost the things that were important to him. He had great family support and resources and went to several different treatment facilities and sober living environments. Burt could maintain abstinence and improve for a few months but then would use again and go into another round of treatment. When he came to our program, we focused on all of the success that he was having, rather than focusing on failures. For the last few years, despite several spectacular and scary failures, Burt has had many more days of success than failures. Working with this idea and plan in mind, he has been continuously better and has regained his family and a new, successful work life.

# Rebecca

Rebecca came to us for opioid dependence. She had started using as a teenager, and had come from a home that experienced a great deal of emotional, physical and sexual abuse. When she was 16 years old, she had caused a motor vehicle accident where the other driver died. In the Intensive group process, she worked a great deal on both guilt and shame. She had guilt over her actions that cost another person their life and shame over the abuse done to her during her childhood. Several times during her work with us, Rebecca would self-destruct and return to use for a few days, but she would return to group and continue the hard work. Her recovery plan involved yoga and individual therapy. The yoga helped to calm her anxiety and the individual therapy addressed issues from the guilt and shame she felt. She has been abstinent for four years.

The importance of sharing the stories from these hard working and courageous people is that their getting better did not involve a straight path with no problems. It is the direction of the arrow to watch, not whether it is a perfect line. The pathways of recovery are seldom a perfect line. Each person's recovery was multifaceted and different from others. What we offered them was the respect to honor their path. Our hope is with more knowledge, we can all do the same.

*Pam and Steve Moore*

# Epilogue

*We can spend our days bemoaning our losses, or we can grow from them.*
*Ultimately the choice is ours. We can be victims of circumstance or masters of our*
*own fate, but make no mistake, we can not be both.*

*Christopher Browne*

I (Pam) stopped attending self-help Alcoholic Anonymous type groups at around five years sober. I worked with a mentor that helped me to step away as it had started becoming destructive for me. I felt lifeless and listless when I attended. I did not stop my recovery process. At first I went to women's book clubs and got involved with church. At one point I got very involved in Catechesis of the Good Shepherd which was a Montessori Sunday School for toddlers and elementary aged children. It involved artwork and a lot of creativity that brought much meaning to my life. I moved on from that as my daughter aged and church lost some of its meaning for me. I went to Recovery Dharma for a while and found it very helpful with learning to stay centered. I have studied the Enneagram and attended multiple workshops and groups to assist with my continued recovery process. I got very involved in some persona work, learning and studying with other people in mental health about fixed false beliefs through Jungian principles.

I have stayed involved in my own personal therapy. Art and journaling have remained throughout my recovery as very big parts of what works for me but even those aspects have changed. I have not picked up a mood-altering substance in over thirty-four years but even today I know to listen to fixed false beliefs and to pay attention to what is going on underneath the surface of me. Recovery did not end but it did morph into something different, and I expect it to keep evolving. The plan changes.

I (Steve) have still attended 12-step programs off and on over the years and more importantly have considered it to be an important part of my recovery process. Over time I discovered breath and body work, and I did a lot of relationship training and work. These were very helpful to me. Most recently I have been very involved in Men's work (specifically Illuman\*) and it has become a very important part of my growth and development. Throughout these, now more than three decades, I have had some terrific therapy from some excellent professionals. Those also have changed over time as my personal wisdom path and journey evolves. The plan changes.

---

\* Illuman is a not for profit organization for men who are simply interested in becoming better, more authentic men.

# Appendix A

■

## The ACES Test

While you were growing up, during your first 18 years of life:

1. Did a parent or other adult in the household often: Swear at you, insult you, put you down, or humiliate you? Or act in a way that made you afraid that you might be physically hurt? Yes/No

If Yes, enter 1 _____

2. Did a parent or other adult in the household often: Push, grab, slap, or throw something at you? Or ever hit you so hard that you had marks or were injured? Yes/No If Yes, enter 1 _____

3. Did an adult or person at least 5 years older than you ever: Touch or fondle you or have you touch their body in a sexual way? Or attempt, or actually have oral, anal, or vaginal intercourse with you? Yes/No If Yes, enter 1 _____

4. Did you often feel that: No one in your family loved you or thought you were important or special? Or Adverse Childhood Experience (ACE) Questionnaire 2, Your family didn't look out for each other, feel close to each other, or support each other? Yes/No If Yes, enter 1 _____

5. Did you often feel that: You didn't have enough to eat, had to wear dirty

clothes, and had no one to protect you? Or your parents were too drunk or high to take care of you or take you to the doctor if you needed it? Yes/No If Yes, enter 1 _____

6. Were your parents ever separated or divorced? Yes/No If Yes, enter 1 _____

7. Were any of your parents or other adult caregivers: Often pushed, grabbed, slapped, or had something thrown at them? Or sometimes or often kicked, bitten, hit with a fist, or hit with something hard? Or ever repeatedly hit over at least a few minutes or threatened with a gun or knife? Yes/No If Yes, enter 1 _____

8. Did you live with anyone who was a problem drinker or alcoholic, or who used street drugs? Yes/No If Yes, enter 1 _____

9. Was a household member depressed or mentally ill, or did a household member attempt suicide? Yes/No If Yes, enter 1 _____

10. Did a household member go to prison? Yes/No If Yes, enter 1 _____

ACE SCORE (Total "Yes" Answers): _____

# Appendix B:
## Resources for Help

### Listing of Different Types of Self-Help Meetings

#### Substance Use Disorders

- Alcoholics Anonymous - https://www.aa.org
- SMART Recovery - https://www.smartrecoverytest.org
- Women for Sobriety - https://womenforsobriety.org
- Recovery Dharma - https://recoverydharma.org
- Refuge Recovery - https://www.refugerecovery.org
- Celebrate Recovery - https://www.celebraterecovery.com
- Chemical Dependents Anonymous - https://www.cdaweb.org
- Cocaine Anonymous - https://ca.org
- Crystal Meth Anonymous - https://wpx.crystalmeth.org
- Pagan In Recovery - http://www.deesigned.net/paganinrecovery
- Drug Addicts Anonymous - https://www.daausa.org
- Life Ring Recovery - https://lifering.org

- Marijuana Anonymous - https://marijuana-anonymous.org
- Moderation Management - https://moderation.org
- Narcotics Anonymous - https://www.na.org
- Pills Anonymous - https://www.pillsanonymous.org

## Sex Addiction

- Sexaholics Anonymous - https://www.sa.org
- Sex and Love Addicts Anonymous - https://slaafws.org
- Sexual Compulsives Anonymous - https://sca-recovery.org
- Sex Addicts Anonymous - https://saa-recovery.org
- Disordered Relationships
- Love Addicts Anonymous - http://www.loveaddicts.org
- Sex and Love Addicts Anonymous - https://slaafws.org

## Support For Those Who Have Been Abused and Have Experienced Trauma

- Survivors of Incest Anonymous - https://siawso.org
- Male Survivors - https://malesurvivor.org
- Gift From Within - https://www.giftfromwithin.org
- Sidran Institute Clearinghouse - https://www.sidran.org
- International Society for the Study of Trauma and Dissociation - https://www.isst-d.org

# Emotional and Mental Health Recovery

- Anxiety and Depression Association - https://adaa.org

- Attention Deficit Disorder Association - https://add.org

- Autism Society - https://www.autism-society.org

- Brain Injury Association - https://www.biausa.org

- Crisis Text Line - https://www.crisistextline.org

- Depression and Bipolar Support - https://www.dbsalliance.org

- International OCD Association - https://iocdf.org

- National Alliance on Mental Illness - https://nami.org

- National Eating Disorders - https://www.nationaleatingdisorders.org

- Asperger's Syndrome - http://www.aspergersyndrome.org

- Body Focused Repetitive Behavior Foundation - www.bfrb.org

- American Association of Suicidology - https://suicidology.org

- The Withdrawal Project - https://withdrawal.theinnercompass.org

# Miscellaneous Problem Behavior Support Groups

- Gamblers Anonymous - http://www.gamblersanonymous.org

- Self-Mutilators Anonymous - https://www.selfmutilatorsanonymous.org

- OverEaters Anonymous - https://oa.org

- Dual Recovery Anonymous - http://www.draonline.org

- Debtors Anonymous - https://debtorsanonymous.org

- Spenders Anonymous - http://www.spenders.org

- Emotions Anonymous - https://emotionsanonymous.org

- Workaholics Anonymous - https://workaholics-anonymous.org

# For Families and Codependents

- SMART Recovery for Families - https://www.smartrecovery.org/family
- PALS Parents of Addicted Loved Ones - https://palgroup.org
- Compassionate Friends - https://www.compassionatefriends.org
- National Federation of Families - https://www.ffcmh.org
- Caregivers Actions - https://caregiveraction.org
- Balanced Mind Parent Network - https://community.dbsalliance.org
- Co-Sex and Love Addicts Anonymous http://coslaa.org
- Adult Children of Alcoholics - https://adultchildren.org
- Al-Anon - https://al-anon.org
- Codependents Anonymous https://coda.org
- Families Anonymous - https://www.familiesanonymous.org
- Nar-Anon - https://www.nar-anon.org
- Recovering Couples Anonymous - https://recovering-couples.org/
- Sex Addicts Anon - https://sanon.org

# References
## Resources for Help

■

## References

### CH 2: The Same but Different

- GORSKI, T. T., (1989). Passages Through Recovery. Center City, MN: Hazelden Press.

- GORSKI, T. T., The CENAPS® Model of Relapse Prevention Planning. In: DALY, D. W., (1989a) Relapse: Conceptual, Research, and Clinical Perspectives. Hayward Press, and J Chem Depend Treat (2)2, 1989a.

- GORSKI, T. T., (1995). Relapse Prevention Therapy Workshop –Managing core personality and lifestyle issues. USA: Herald House/Independence Press.

- GORSKI, T. T., KELLEY. J. M., (2007). Counsellor's Manual for Relapse Prevention with Chemically Dependent Criminal Offenders. [online]. Available from: http://www6dotXEQscy_WKOZOHPexJMruJSLfyLaT6-Jy/Hybrid%20Unit%2011/Gorski%27s%20Manual.pdf [Accessed 31 Jan 2008].

- GOSSOP, M., STEWART, D., BROWNE, N. MARSDEN, J. (2002). Factors associated with abstinence, lapse or relapse to heroin use after residential treatment: protective effect of coping responses. Addiction, 97(10), pp.1259-67.

- LARIMER, M. E., PALMER, R. S., MARLATT, G. A., (1999). Relapse Prevention –An overview of Marlatt's Cognitive-Behavioral Model. Alcohol

Research & Health, 23 (2), pp151-159.

- MARLATT, G. A., & DONOVAN, D. M., eds. (2005). Relapse Prevention – Maintenance strategies in the treatment of addictive behaviors, 2nded. New York: Guilford Press.

- MARLATT,G. A., & GORDON, J. R., (1985). 1st Relapse Prevention: Maintenance strategies in the treatment of addictive behaviors, New York: Guilford Press.McLEOD, J., (2003). 3rd An introduction to counselling. Glasgow: Open University Press.

- MILLER, W. R., HARRIS, R. J. (2000). A simple scale of Gorski's warning signs for relapse. [online] PMID: 11022817 [PubMed -indexed for MEDLINE]. Available from: http://www.ncbi.nlm.nih.gov/sites/entrez?WebEnv=0r5F7E8VcQU9vTmwUuUx9TcccDL7UQZY450Tym-06Mgve0P07TCLy%40mqZUwIIOFkQAAHxgrkIAAAAV&db=pubmed&orig_db=pubmed&term=gorski%20paws&cmd=search&cmd_current=&query_key=1&dopt=AbstractPlus&dispmax=20&sort=&SendTo=&filt[Accessed 30 Jan 2008].

- PROCHASKA, J. O., & DiCLEMENTE, C. C., (1986) Toward a comprehensive model of change, In MILLER, W. R., & HEATHER, N. Eds., Treating Addictive Behaviors: Process of change. pp. 3-27. New York: Plenum.

- RILEY, D. M., SOBELL, L. C., LEO, G. I., SOBELL, M. B., KLAJNER, F., (1987). Behavioral treatment of alcohol problems; a review and a comparison of behavioral and non-behavioral studies. In: Treatment and prevention of alcohol problems: a resource manual. New York: Academic Press.

# CH 3: RAW: Ready, Able, Willing

- Anderson DJ, McGovern JP, DuPont RL. The origins of the Minnesota model of addiction treatment--a first person account. J Addict Dis. 1999;18(1):107-14. doi: 10.1300/J069v18n01_10. PMID: 10234566.

- Jellinek, E. M., "Phases in the Drinking History of Alcoholics: Analysis of a Survey Conducted by the Official Organ of Alcoholics Anonymous", Quarterly Journal of Studies on Alcohol, Vol.7, (1946), pp. 1–88.

- Prochaska, JO . Systems of Psychotherapy: A Transtheoretical Analysis. 2nd ed. Pacific Grove, California: Brooks-Cole, 1984.

- Miller, WR; Heather, N. (eds.). Treating addictive behaviors. 2nd ed. New York: Plenum Press; 1998. ISBN 0-306-45852-7.

- Velasquez, MM. Group treatment for substance abuse: a stages-of-change therapy manual. New York: Guilford Press; 2001. ISBN 1-57230-625-4.

- DeWit DJ, Adlaf EM, Offord DR, Ogborne AC. Age at first alcohol use: a risk factor for the development of alcohol disorders. Am J Psychiatry. 2000 May;157(5):745-50. doi: 10.1176/appi.ajp.157.5.745. PMID: 10784467.

- The adolescent brain: Beyond raging hormones - Harvard Health

- https://www.health.harvard.edu/mind-and-mood/the-adolescent-brain-beyond-raging-hormones. Published: March, 2011

- NIDA. 2021, April 19. What are marijuana's effects? Retrieved from https://www.drugabuse.gov/publications/research-reports/marijuana/what-are-marijuana-effects on 2021, May 2

## CH 6: Genetics

- NIDA. 2019, August 5. Genetics and Epigenetics of Addiction Drug Facts. Retrieved from https://www.drugabuse.gov/publications/drugfacts/genetics-epigenetics-addiction on 2021, May 2

- AGRAWAL, A., AND LYNSKEY, M. The genetic epidemiology of cannabis use, abuse and dependence. Addiction 101:801–812, 2006. PMID: 16696624

- DICK, D.M.; PLUNKETT, J.; WETHERILL, L.F.; ET AL. Association between GABRA1 and drinking behaviors in the Collaborative Study on the

Genetics of Alcoholism sample. Alcoholism: Clinical and Experimental Research 30:1101–1110, 2006b. PMID: 16792556

- HILL, S.Y.; SHEN, S.; ZEZZA, N.; ET AL. A genome wide search for alcoholism susceptibility genes. American Journal of Medical Genetics Part B: Neuropsychiatric Genetics 128B:102–113, 2004. PMID: 15211641

- XUEI, X.; FLURY-WETHERILL, L.; BIERUT, L.; ET AL. The opioid system in alcohol and drug dependence: Family-based association study. American Journal of Medical Genetics Part B: Neuropsychiatric Genetics 144(7):877–884, 2007. PMID: 17503481

## CH 7: Frequency Intensity Duration

- https://www.drugpolicyfacts.org/chapter/addictive_properties#sthash.S4nT2tJ2.dpbs

- https://www.americanscientist.org/sites/americanscientist.org/files/200645104835_307.pdf

## CH 8: Co-Existing Disorders

- Murthy P, Chand P. Treatment of dual diagnosis disorders. Curr Opin Psychiatry. 2012 May;25(3):194-200. doi: 10.1097/YCO.0b013e328351a3e0. PMID: 22395768.

- Brenner P, Brandt L, Li G, DiBernardo A, Bodén R, Reutfors J. Substance use disorders and risk for treatment resistant depression: a population-based, nested case-control study. Addiction. 2020 Apr;115(4):768-777. doi: 10.1111/add.14866. Epub 2019 Dec 16. PMID: 31656053; PMCID: PMC7078870.

- https://www.ptsd.va.gov/understand/related/substance_misuse.asp

- Souza, T., & Spates, C. R. (2008). Treatment of PTSD and substance abuse comorbidity. The Behavior Analyst Today, 9(1), 11-26. http://dx.doi.org/10.1037/h0100643

- https://www.psycom.net/depression-substance-abuse. 101759-000_AAP_OpioidCrisis_Factsheet_National_v15r6.indd

## Substance Use Disorders in Patients with Anxiety Disorders

- September 6, 2011. Matt G. Kushner, PhD , Sheila M. Specker, MD. Psychiatric Times, Psychiatric Times Vol 28 No 9, Volume 28, Issue 9

- Patrick Köck, Marc Walter. Personality disorder and substance use disorder – An update, Mental Health & Prevention. Volume 12, 2018, Pages 82-89. ISSN 2212-6570, https://doi.org/10.1016/j.mhp.2018.10.003.

- Links PS, Heslegrave RJ, Mitton JE, van Reekum R, Patrick J. Borderline personality disorder and substance abuse: consequences of comorbidity. Can J Psychiatry. 1995 Feb;40(1):9-14. doi: 10.1177/070674379504000105. PMID: 7874683.

- Grant BF, Goldstein RB, Saha TD, et al. Epidemiology of DSM-5 Alcohol Use Disorder: Results from the National Epidemiologic Survey on Alcohol and Related Conditions III. JAMA Psychiatry. 2015;72(8):757–766. doi:10.1001/jamapsychiatry.2015.0584

- L. Sher, Depression and alcoholism, QJM: An International Journal of Medicine, Volume 97, Issue 4, April 2004, Pages 237–240, https://doi.org/10.1093/qjmed/hch045

- Crippa, Jose & Zuardi, Antonio & Martín-Santos, Rocio & Bhattacharyya, Sagnik & Atakan, Zerrin & Mcguire, Philip & Fusar-Poli, Paolo. (2009). Cannabis and anxiety: A critical review of the evidence. Human psycho-pharmacology. 24. 515-23. 10.1002/hup.1048.

- NIDA. 2021, April 13. Is there a link between marijuana use and psychiatric disorders? https://www.drugabuse.gov/publications/research-reports/marijuana/there-link-between-marijuana-use-psychiatric-disorders on 2021, May 2

## Trauma and Addiction

- Peirce, Jessica & Burke, Christopher & Stoller, Kenneth & Neufeld, Karin & Brooner, Robert. (2009). Assessing Traumatic Event Exposure: Comparing the Traumatic Life Events Questionnaire to the Structured Clinical Interview for DSM-IV. Psychological assessment. 21. 210-8. 10.1037/a0015578.

- https://pubs.niaaa.nih.gov/publications/arh23-4/256-262.pdf

## Addiction and Crime

- Drug Use and Dependence, State and Federal Prisoners, 2004, NCJ 213530, October 2006

- Substance Abuse and Treatment, State and Federal Prisoners, 1997, NCJ 172871, January 1999.

- https://drugabusestatistics.org/

## CH 9: Consequences

- https://www.psychologytoday.com/us/articles/200702/toxic-brew

- It Will Never Happen to Me . Claudia Black. (Medical Administration Press, 1982)

- Safe Passage: Recovery for Adult Children of Alcoholics. Stephanie Brown. (John Wiley & Sons, 1992)

- A Place Called Self: Women, Sobriety and Radical Transformation. Stephanie Brown. (Hazelden, 2004)

- A Place Called Self: A Companion Workbook. Stephanie Brown. (Hazelden, 2006)

- Guide to Recovery, A Book for Adult Children of Alcoholics. H. Gravitz and J. Bowden. (Health Communications, 1985)

## CH 10: Physical Issues and Addiction

- https://www.niaaa.nih.gov/publications/brochures-and-fact-sheets/alcohol-facts-and-statistics#:~:text=Alcohol-Related%20Deaths%3A%20An%20estimated%2095%2C000%205%20people%20%28approximately,second%20is%20poor%20diet%20and%20physical%20inactivity.%206

- NIDA. 2021, April 13. What are the medical complications of chronic heroin use? Retrieved from https://www.drugabuse.gov/publications/research-reports/heroin/what-are-medical-complications-chronic-heroin-use on 2021, May 2

- NIDA. 2020, July 13. Addiction and Health. Retrieved from https://www.drugabuse.gov/publications/drugs-brains-behavior-science-addiction/addiction-health on 2021, March 28

- Miller WR, Harris RJ. A simple scale of Gorski's warning signs for relapse. J Stud Alcohol. 2000 Sep;61(5):759-65. doi: 10.15288/jsa.2000.61.759. PMID: 11022817.

- Three Circles. https://saa-recovery.org/literature/three-circles-defining-sexual-sobriety-in-saa/